# The Only Place
# We Live

# The Only Place We Live

Words by
AUGUST DERLETH
JESSE STUART
ROBERT E. GARD

Edited by
MARK E. LEFEBVRE

Wood Engravings by
FRANK UTPATEL

Wisconsin House

iv

First Edition
ISBN 0-88361-040-X

Library of Congress Card Number 76-13755

# ACKNOWLEDGEMENTS

Grateful acknowledgement is made to the Estate of August Derleth
for permission to quote freely from his published works.
Forrest D. Hartmann, Executor, was most encouraging and helpful
throughout the project.
Special thanks go to April Derleth Smith and Walden Derleth
for their cooperation.
Hugo Schwenker and Rick Meng contributed invaluably
by sharing their appreciation of August Derleth
and the world he lived in.

The Wisconsin Academy of Sciences, Arts, and Letters is recognized
for the Utpatel Exhibit it sponsored
which was the catalyst for this book.
Appreciation is extended to James Batt,
Executive Director of the Academy.

Robert E. Gard would like to express his indebtedness to Erma Graeber
for the idea of the story about fighting the Battle of Shiloh
in the lower forty.

# CONTENTS

# PREFACE

The linchpin of THE ONLY PLACE WE LIVE is the art of Frank Utpatel.
The words of August Derleth, Jesse Stuart and Robert E. Gard
have a power and relationship of their own,
but read with the wood engravings they have a deeper affect,
a verbal and visual affect.
The art unifies the observations of the three writers.

The art was the beginning point of THE ONLY PLACE WE LIVE.
I began with the wood engravings and singled out those
which had previously appeared in books by August Derleth.
I then selected passages from these fourteen books
which worked with the individual engravings.
The Derleth section is arranged chronologically
and should give the reader an appreciation
of both Derlteh's and Utpatel's growing and changing vision.

I then sent the other wood engravings on
to Jesse Stuart and Robert E. Gard
and asked them to respond to the art in their own way.
I edited the Stuart section
with regard for his sensitivity to the seasons.
The Gard section emerged as a moving story
with illustrations rather than the shorter,
meditative observations of Derleth and Stuart.

Collectively, I feel we have moved closer to understanding
the possibilities of the places where we live;
we are pleased to share them
within the framework of this book.

Mark E. Lefebvre

A man is worth most to himself and to others,
whether as an observer, or poet, or neighbor, or friend,
where he is most himself,
most contented and at home.
There his life is the most intense and he loses the fewest moments.
Familiar and surrounding objects are the best symbols
and illustrations of his life . . . .
The poet has made the best roots in his native soil of any man,
and is the hardest to transplant.
The man who is often thinking
that it is better to be somewhere else than where he is
excommunicates himself.
If a man is rich and strong anywhere,
it must be on his native soil.

Henry David Thoreau

# The Only Place
# We Live

ATMOSPHERE OF HOUSES/1939

EACH HOUSE stands apart; yet each house belongs in some intangible fashion to its neighbor, and together they belong to one another, for they are the towns. . . .

Then one day I greeted them and they answered in such kind voices, that I stood and gazed after them in wonder that these two women should be mad.

THERE WAS a house along the way to town where a cobbler had once lived. I remember him only dimly . . . . He was nearly always the same, even in dress, for I cannot recall ever having seen him in other than a cobbler's apron, with an awl in one hand and a shoe in the other.

CAUGHT CLOSE to the ground, the house where my maternal grandmother lived brooded in an atmosphere of secrecy.

The house had witnessed all manner of births, marriages, and deaths before I was here to know. There was an air of oppressing age about the house, clinging to its every part, and with this was the haunting suggestion of secrets long lost behind its tranquil walls.

Quiet and bland the house seemed, and yet from about its eaves and corners crept an atmosphere of taunting mystery.

I felt always a sense of peace fraught from the distant past with events of violence, permeated by night-whispers of people already remote in the memory of my white-haired grandmother, whose gentle eyes regarded me in much the same manner as I imagine the house itself looked upon me. There was suffering in her eyes, and there was suffering in the walls of the house, but there was peace in both, the tranquil peace that follows in the wake of suffering. They brooded together, the house and my grandmother, and had silent communication with each other.

They had lived, these two, and their somnolent peace was the peace of aging years.

THERE WAS about the house where my paternal grandparents lived a newness that was in itself old. It lay perhaps in the knowledge that this house had usurped the place of another, older one, and that it had not quite dispelled the atmosphere of that other house. Perhaps, too, the old buildings that surrounded it helped to keep alive in this house the older atmosphere, keeping it alive so long that the house took to itself some of this older atmosphere, becoming one with it.

The atmosphere of the house that had once stood there had impregnated my grandparents, and especially my grandmother, from whom this older atmosphere flowed into all corners of the new house.

My grandmother was often seen in the garden . . . . Her year was not marked by calendar months, but by flowers and their blossom time. March she knew by the squills, April by the violets and anemones, May by the lilies-of-the-valley and the lilacs, June by the sweet Williams and the roses. Thus it was with her. December, January, and February saw her greatest life within the house, and in these months the house, its windows colored, brought alive by geraniums and other winter plants, seemed to overcome for a brief time the atmosphere of that other older house which lurked always so near.

These two living alone in the house, so much older than the house, carried with them the atmosphere of that other, and an atmosphere of the town when young, the pioneer town, and with these they moulded the house, pressing these upon the house, so that its newness was lost, its own atmosphere gradually coming to assume that of the other.

I remember this house for an atmosphere of twilight peace in later years, an atmosphere coming from the often seen picture of these two old pioneers sitting at table to a meager meal in the soft dusk, their eyes watching the sun, night after night, in its slow descent beyond the horizon, watching the afterglow being drawn away from the darkening sky.

THE KRAFT house thrown proudly across a flowing soft green lawn, was cold. A wire fence shut it away from the rest of the town, a fence precisely made to enclose the Kraft estate. The red brick and white stone of the house seemed to absorb no warmth. The windows were closed eyes; the gables condescended to look out upon the village; the doors were prim, severe; the spaced trees straight and tall on the lawn. And yet the house was new, and its pride was false.

Darkness laid siege to the pride and chill of the brick and stone, employing the trees to press their shadows close upon the house, to banish the fence into the darkest places, and the moonlight silvered the roof, the gables and the window-eyes, webbing the lawn, the trees and the house itself. Its aloofness vanquished, the house fell gently into the atmosphere of the town.

I REMEMBER the Obrecht house, stately and aloof, its blinds closed over its deep-set windows, an air of closepressing kindly hauteur clinging about its gaunt white stories flung against the trees and sky. It was very old, yet so solidly built that its age was only felt and seldom seen.

In later years some easterners bought the house and sought to beautify it by the addition of stone gates, privet hedges, and a large brick porch over the lily-of-the-valley beds, which were thus destroyed. The house was cold to them, divorced itself from these new things, and retained its older atmosphere, so that in time it seemed as if the gates, the hedges, and the porch were cast off things long fallen into decay, with the old house standing proudly, scornfully aloof from them.

Always it seemed that in its shadowed rooms the long dead Obrechts still wandered, in its corridors the tap of Christian Obrecht's cane still sounded, and in the forgetful darkness of the night the stairs creaked and laughed with the Obrecht children, whose long lost cries of joy still rang in the aging rafters of the house.

IMPOSED UPON the Lazar house was the spirit of the long dead Mrs. Lazar, the childless old lady, stern and forbidding, cold and withdrawn from the world, whose years had been spent in the house from her marriage to her death. Only beyond the shadow of her phantom self could the house assume its atmosphere.

It was restless under the brooding intensity of her deathless spirit. It sought, as it had long sought, to crush the atmosphere she had imposed, and supplant it with its own, a gentle, somnolent air of quiet peace.

Thus the house remains in my memory, a house outwardly cold, inwardly struggling with the tenacious atmosphere left to dominate by the old lady whose spectral figure lingers to haunt its declining years.

THERE ARE many houses, and their combined atmospheres make up the atmosphere of my town. There are so many tranquil, peaceful houses, and their quiet helps subdue the atmosphere of houses that cry aloud in tragedy . . . .

The atmosphere is one of moving peace, a quiet where from far below faint stirrings can be heard, a pool in a deep forest, where seldom ripples come to disturb its placid surface; the atmosphere of my town is like this pool, save that disturbing ripples surge upward from below, from the depths of this atmospheric pool, surge upward from time past, lost a while in present time, and gone again.

VILLAGE YEAR/1941

2 JANUARY: After an all night's snowfall, with the sky still leaden and snow coming down, the temperature close to thirty, I went this afternoon into the marshes, and was lost at once in a dim, strange world, every bush and tree and weed hung heavy with the damp, clinging flakes, snow piled two inches high on every limb, bending cedars and pines low with its weight, capping teasel and mullein, dogbane and climbing false buckwheat pods. No path was broken in the foot-deep snow, and hidden drifts made walking difficult and treacherous, but no less exhilarating. No sound among the trees, an almost unnatural silence prevailed, and the air was fresh and alive with the fragrance of wet snow. With trees pressing close and snow limiting vision, there was a feeling of limitless depth; it was as if the snow-hung trees and shrubs cut me away from Sac Prairie and all the world beyond, the falling flakes and the pattern of limbs against the gray sky endlessly interwoven without visible boundaries, without even small units, so deceptive was the wall of snow to the eye.

Even in the deep woods, little sound came to ear: the sliding of snow from an overloaded limb, the rustling of flakes among dry leaves still clinging to oak trees along the way, the occasional snap of a branch broken by the snow's weight, and subdued voices of wildlife—kinglets, snow buntings, quail—and once the sudden rising of a jacksnipe from the brookside where it had been feeding, doubtless, at the water's edge. The brook's murmuring came muffled. Walking here with scarcely more noise than a woodland creature's footfalls in the deep snow, I made nevertheless enough diversion to startle a year-old buck, which rose up suddenly in a clump of prickly ash and black alder bushes, still red with their hollylike fruit, less than thirty feet away.

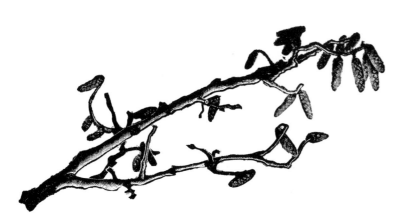

13 JANUARY: Early this afternoon the flutelike phe-be-be of the chickadees sounded in the village, plaintive and welcome to the ear. And in the harness shop, March became tangible where the soft silver-gray catkins of Hugh's pussywillows, set against the back window, had broken their sheaths. . . .

"When my second husband died, I sat at the window in the early morning, and I looked out, and I asked myself: 'Are you going to make it?' Now I ask myself that every morning, and I know I am."

11 FEBRUARY: I walked down and watched farmer Hornung haul cut wood from the meadow to the road past the Triangle . . . . He is a good, earthy fellow, simple-minded and honest, far better than many other villagers, who live under a veneer of transparently thin culture and conduct themselves tacitly as overlords of man and beast. I could not help thinking how small he looked, how symbolic was his smallness in the field, symbolic of man against all earth, against nature . . . .

**Man Track Here**

Less than this my lone path is:
a deermouse track in winter's snow—
less than any mark of hare or crow.
Than the least falling leaf from the most crabbed, most
    aged tree
in the least wind, than the least pebble dropped into
    the stillest pool,
than the most secret ways of the foolish, obscure bee,
no path of mine is now as much, nothing of mine is
more. Through wood, way over meadow and plain,
footprint on hill and river sand, by moonlight and by
    rain,
where laboringly my clear path went, there
lordly strides now windy snow, and where
my challenge sounded to the wind, now looms the
    blank, unheeding air.

24 AUGUST: In the darkness over Bergen's Island and on the trestle over the east channel of the Wisconsin, I stood tonight to pick out of the darkness a multitude of smells I might not have known in the afterglow: the smell of wet river sand, of the water itself, of old wood exposed by the falling water-level, of bridge timbers and cinders; and of sounds: rustling in the grasses, insects humming past, frogs jumping off the embankment, bird cheepings, crickets, katydids. And along the embankment beyond rose the sweetness of Joe-Pye weed, the heady fragrance of the parasitic dodder clinging to helianthus stalks, the rich miasma of the Spring Slough and the meadow. Mallards worked in the water there, a muskrat plunged in and away, and a slithering in the grass may have been a snake. The senses seem to be more alert in darkness.

I went on down the embankment, and in the night's mysterious dark-light, heard the brook's voice: a faint murmuring, magnified in the darkness, and the rustling of grasses and leaves where water passed, the quick running patter of a bird along the brook's edge—possibly a solitary sandpiper—the guttural croaking of bullfrogs, and on Lenson's Meadow saw a few fireflies still.

2 SEPTEMBER: A still, beautiful night, darkness alive with subdued cries of nighthawks, whippoor-wills, owls, Hylidae, a lone killdeer, the stridulations of katydids and crickets, and the krark, krark of a great blue heron winging its way upriver. In the hills dogs barked, and beside the railroad tracks along the embankment across the Wisconsin, lesser creatures made their secret scuttering in passing among grass and leaves. I walked down the rail-road, crossing opposite the Triangle to sit on the pasture gate beside the highway and watch the moon rise redly over the cornfield, its light slant-ing down the cornrows and over the road: a deep yellow light, almost golden at first, changing to a strange green-white glow in the late summer haze when the moon had risen higher. Not far south of the moon, Fomalhaut shone. Dwelling upon this scene, I wrote **Harvest Moon** by moonlight.

Out of the evening haze,
out of the apple smell,
plum smell, fragrance of corn,
the moon comes up:
great, round, orange,
like a smoke god,
a pumpkin god,
like something Indians forgot,
left to be born again:
comes up behind the old rail fence,
the elm bent over, cornshocks
row on row in the stubble field.
In deep grass the crickets mourn,
the katydids sing; along the distant lane
the threshers' whistle pipes;
and cornleaves rustle and murmur,
murmur and rustle without wind.

Over the hills,
out of the smoky haze
the moon comes,
after Andromeda, after Aries,
after the summer gone:
over the cornshocks
rises and hangs
ripe as apples sweet in air,
mellow as plums down pasture's edge;
under the maple, under the ash,
hangs under elm's spread limb.
Among the oak's gnarled boughs
leaves break away
one by one, drift, fall without wound
at the year's ripe touch.

Pale yellow light, pale lemon sheen,
smoky and dim,
orange gone to ochre and yellow, moon
hangs with its light
slanted down hills, down cornrows,
old fence:
softens the stubble,
soothes the old wood,
over all earth, over all water
says: how beautiful
in dying,
how beautiful is death!

After half an hour, I went up the Mazomanie road and lost the moon behind the low Ganser Hills, but all the time there was that secret glow against which the gnarled oaks ranged from the hillslopes to the sky, the far stars above, and fragrance in the air: of dodder, hay, cut corn, the cloying miasma of the lowlands. Passing a dip in the hills, I saw the moon begin to rise and stood to watch it, waiting until its light slanted down the slopes, the orange glow of it in the haze topping into whiteness beyond the hills with a strange, secret glory: so that I watched it rise again and again, moving forward and back so that I might see this miracle of beauty repeated anew, each time a little farther up the slope, each time behind different trees: the orange glow rising, the yellow-white moon, the hidden life among the trees, dark and still in the moon's brightness.

3 OCTOBER: For the first time in this season, I was conscious today in the village of the fragrance of leaves, the definite autumn odors rising from fallen leaves, noticing this particularly about soft maple foliage, the dry and decaying leaves of which have a soft, cloying sweetness, in contrast to the smoke-pungence of oak leaves a little later. These two: maple and oak: among common trees in Sac Prairie have the strongest, most easily identified odor. In the woods nothing is stronger than the sycamore's amazing, smoky odor or the prickly ash's minty fragrance. Acorns crack under foot today, and make a hollow sound striking roofs as they fall.

I spent the afternoon in the marshes, walking slowly down the railroad tracks. The evidence of autumn was everywhere today—Virginia creeper a bright red, with scarlet, crimson, maroon in its foliage; poison ivy pale pink, mottled and yellow red; maples, elms, birch, poplars, cottonwoods, and willows all shedding yellow leaves; the common sumac burning vermilion: and against this brightness, the wayside color of berries, hanging heavy still—dark blue wild grapes, black-blue bunches of carrion berries and Virginia creeper, black berries of the sweet elder, the last of silky cornel's pale blue berries, the fruit of asparagus hanging redly among its feathery branches, now yellowing and browning, maroon smooth sumac fruit, the roundleaf greenbriar's dark blue berries, the unbroken sheaths of orange bittersweet, the green-white berries of poison ivy, the heavy pendant fruit of the true Solomon's Seal in single rows along the underside of stems, the red to purple cluster of berries atop the false spikenard, the cerise fruit of the wahoo or spindle tree.

Leaves today: golden, green, brown, rose, maroon: lay upon the still, unmoving surfaces of ponds and sloughs, with the afternoon sunlight falling athwart the water and the colorful woods beyond; and a great blue heron stood one-legged on the edge of the Spring Slough, the epitome of autumn.

11 OCTOBER: In the marshes this evening with Hugh, heard a solitary cricket frog near the Ice Slough. Already the frogs are moving inland, making ready for winter. Standing there to listen, we heard also the distant nostalgic whistle of a steam engine sounding from the prairie west of river and village. The smell of corn leaves lay in clouds here and there along the railroad. At the pasture gate across from the Lower Meadow, we stood to hear a fox yawp; he called three times, in cries to the number of six or seven each time, a strange, sometimes eerie sound; but after three rounds of cries, he was silent.

13 NOVEMBER: In the bottoms this afternoon, with a cold wind roaring through the trees, the brook was so black with minnows that every concerted movement resulted in many of them being forced in a wave from the water, making a silver movement along the brook's banks. Over the Lower Meadow's north line the maples were thick with maroon buds, and the birch's long fingerlike buds waved gracefully in the wind, sheathing the coming spring. All along the meadow seeds were beautiful: bladder nut, wahoo, climbing false buckwheat, carrion berries, black alders, and the fragile whiskery woodbine seeds. The mustard of pussywillows and the red of osiers made the distances colorful; here and there the steel blue of silky cornel berries caught the sun.

17 DECEMBER: The early wintry days of late autumn begin the old harness-shop season; for three months now Hugh and his father—long ago in early boyhood days dubbed Eli, or Alias the Night Wind—will be busy oiling and repairing harnesses for farmers, whose ceaseless work on the land severe weather and heavy snows bring to a brief respite. Though it stands on Water Street, surrounded by neon signs and modern fronts (most of them a bastard Venetian with German behinds), the old harness shop continues to hold about it a mellow atmosphere of time past, with its shuttered front, its numerous small sheds adjoining the building in the rear, the open stairway up the north wall to the second story, where lived until recently Long John, the Sage of Water Street, and where now Nick holds forth, repairing all kinds of gadgets, at which he is dexterous, and in the dusk playing his fiddle.

Inside, it is mellow with age, redolent with the smell of old leather, wax, and oils. The walls are decorated with calendars from many a year, their pleasant colorful old pictures quaint today and yet not a far cry from the shop's own calendars on the counter near the door, as always at this time of the year. Higher on the walls, hooks hold stoutly made harnesses; Eli (whose name is really, prosaically Bill) made most of them, and now Hugh, too, helps to make them. Here and there are factory products, but these can never bear too close a scrutiny beside the immeasurably superior hand-worked harnesses. The first few of the season's repaired and oiled harnesses hang from long rows of hooks in the ceiling beyond the old stoves, and behind them, the newly red-painted hames are strung up to dry. Constantly in this season Hugh and Eli are at work along the crude but efficient workbench under the window on the north wall, or at the secondary "leather" workbench along the south wall, where no window is, and green-shaded globes must furnish light by which to work. From the north bench, Hugh can look out up the aging shingled roof of the little red-brick Fuchs house, almost upon the shop, with room only for a single passageway between at one place, past the rooftop to the Lachmund house gable and the old elms against the winter's blue sky.

31 DECEMBER: My footsteps upon the hard snow like the clock's sound marking Sac Prairie's years as minutes down the frozen air before another year, another year, and still another year. . . .

FU

AND YOU THOREAU/1944

**Walker-Errant**

Whether it is Concord or Sac Prairie,
Walden or Wisconsin's shore,
Taos or Deadwood or Bad Axe or
Santa Fe where goes the walker solitary
in woods, past yucca bloom,
the redwood tree and sycamore,
the forest stream, the pool, he goes there
as once Thoreau walked in flesh, in heart—

in quiet like an unstirred fern within the wood,
at ocean's stir and ceaseless edge,
in untinged and vacant desert air . . .

   "I wish to speak a word
     for Nature, for freedom absolute
     and wildness . . ."

—of mild and stately deer, unquiet bird,
of toad with basilisk eye and turtle mute
on summer's slough-bound log,
the west side of the wood, the evening's side,
with sun roseate, magenta there,
and the secret thrush singing
in hushed air . . .

"The most alive is wildest,
  not yet subdued to man,
  and all good things are wild . . ."

—as dark reflecting waters, where the loon,
the habitant, and owls cry
under the evening's rind of moon . . .

Fox across the pond on snow,
fox in the sun on rim of hill,
fox stalking in the dark the noiseless whippoorwill,
careless of his freedom in the blow
of shad . . .

  "I give him sun,
  I give him earth,
  as to their true proprietor . . .

  Life consists with wildness."

Sonoita, Arroyo Hondo, Grand Portage, Cibicute,
Horse Shoe Canyon, Biwabik—each some mute
Thoreau's Walden, where walkers-errant
hold hope in quaking swamps, sand's mirage,
in painted mountains, pine-sweet air—

Man, the transient habitant, a parcel and a part
of Nature which alone remains, is whole.

  "I wish to speak a word
  for Nature, for freedom absolute,
  and wildness . . ."

What is it in such places
where willows bend, the face
of heaven looks up from the lilies and the rippled water,
where wild plum blooms, and the looming wind
walks in the grasses
where the blue racer passes,
jewels in his head?

What is it answers the unquiet questions
laired in the stirred, unquiet, ambushed heart?

  "I wish to speak a word
  for Nature, for freedom absolute . . ."

**Wild Apples**
Thoreau in the Midwest: May, 1861

Calamus budded in the bottomland,
the lilacs blooming, and the wild crabapple:
rivers swollen with water from the north,
snow water, and the whippoorwills,
as once before, sing in the dusk . . .

Eighty years since he crossed Wisconsin
into Minnesota, along wild rivers—
cold to the council of the Sioux
at Redwood, who had expected to be warmed:
cold to the flash and show,
cold even to the Little Crow
exchanging words with him.—Thoreau!
Thoreau dying.

The Mississippi indolent with late spring:
country of larks, redwings, hawks,
wild pigeons, where he hunted nests
and gophers, and at last—
lo! the wild crabapple!

"Half-fabulous to me . . .
I began to notice from the cars a tree
with handsome rose-colored flowers.
Eight miles west of the Falls,
I touched it, smelled it,
secured a lingering corymbe of the flowers,
remarkable for their delicious odor . . ."

Sweet on the air, crabapple,
wild crabapple cloud of pink on country lane,
on rind of hill:

       "Indigenous,
        like the Indians . . ."
              The May wind
in their branches, moonlight
white in the enlarging whiteness of the night
on the rose corymbs—
his footsteps passing,
spectral, hushed sound in muted air; touching,
smelling—lover of bird, wood, sky—
(with one year left in which to die).

Fifth Month again. Where now
I walk beneath the old new-leafing bough—
underfoot bergamotte, the violet,
picking morels where I go—
upon the air the wild perfume,
the pink crab's bloom,
the tree an alien visitation at the line-fence—
I think of him, Thoreau.

The wild, indigenous American tree,—
so it must have seemed to him,
the indigenous American,
the man forever young . . .

       "Not an assured inhabitant of earth . .
        not quite earthy . . something tender
        and divine about him."

—words clinging to the mind
like scent far-scattered by the heart
of Thoreau, Thoreau dying, his feet on earth
last, lingering, to trace the trackless
path into the enormous last unseen wonder,
hearing the bees' sound, the killdeer's crying,
hearing the heart of the continent beating
in the sweet land,
he walked, dying.

> "Not an assured inhabitant of earth . .
> not quite earthy . . something tender
> and divine about him. . . . Indigenous,
> like the Indians . . ."

". . a lingering corymb of the flowers:"
—so with scent the heart bemusing
another generation's hours.

Lilacs in the dooryards,
in the deep woods, spikenard;
in the bottoms budded
calamus, and water-lilies yellow on the sloughs;
at field's edge, the pasture line,
wood's rim, the tawny tree,
the cloud of pink against unclouded sky,
as eighty years gone by . . .

> "Half-fabulous to me . .
> I began to notice from the cars a tree
> with handsome rose-colored flowers . ."

HABITANT OF DUSK/1946

## A Letter To Someone Loved

(At the brook.
Twelve noon, by the sun.)

I send you this hour,
and the south wind blowing;
I send you hawk turning on the slopes of air,
and sun in the sienna grasses;
I send you the out-of-season frog growing
sluggish on the bank, and the late-blooming flower . . .

And, because I think you care,
I send myself, minute and plain,
waiting humbly between happiness and pain,
where neither is forever done.

**The Nectar Seekers**

Invading the wild phlox
under Venus and the waxing moon,
dreamlike flitting, flower to flower,
the Sphinx-moths. The hour,
of dusk: the time, between soon
and forever.

The violated heart cradles the myth,
the image, you—unheard,
unseen in evening air,

(Name—a word like the voice of a secret bird:
eyes—young as oncoming night is young,
as stars, as flowers on the bright edge of night:
the arms remembered like the hushed wind
        passing by,
poignant as a muted cry!)

and, watching there, becomes aware
of kinship with these soundless fluttering moths,
but earthbound, unwinged among the rocks
of pain remembered, under an eternal moon,
between forever, alas! and perhaps soon . . .

Ah, the habitants of dusk, the Sphinx-moths
as in and of a dream, and the plain
man alone with foreknown pain—
kin—the nectar-seekers . . .

VILLAGE DAYBOOK/1947

17 JANUARY: What I said stirred Emmy to remember Daisy Vellairs, who, she said, had lived in a house near Grandfather Derleth's place, and was a woman in middle age when Emmy had known her, a little touched, with the habit of coming to the threshold of her porch and talking to the birds. "Sing, you birds," she would cry out.

6 JANUARY: I walked on down to the second brook, seeing how the water had risen to stand over a fourth of Lenson's Meadow, and there turned and went leisurely back, taking delight in the brightness of lichens on the trees, and the white and grey of early pussywillows.

13 FEBRUARY: The skunk cabbages were out today—and the redwings. I heard redwing song while I stood on the brook trestle this afternoon, and, thinking that starlings were at their imitations, I did not turn; but, presently, the cries persisting, and not broken by other half-uttered calls, I looked around and found the three birds without difficulty, swinging in the topmost branches of the maple trees along the second brook, and quite clearly redwings, as I ascertained by walking down to the second brook trestle and examining the birds at closer range. Whether they were winter residents or the first of the migrants, there was no way of knowing. If of winter, they remained well hidden since autumn, to have been brought out for the first time by the temperature of forty above today. If of spring, the oldsters will gravely foretell an early spring from their appearance. They were not alarmed at my presence, but kept on calling until I crossed to the Mazomanie road and walked up to that place along the highway where the skunk cabbages grow. Scores of them were well above the ground, one or two actually in bloom, yellow pollen on their purplish spathes shielded by their green-mauve sheaths, as if impervious to cold. Distantly, the redwings still called, and from the hill slopes on the far side of the road came the pleasant music of rills flowing down from the snow banks athwart the hills, two uncertain and brief voices of spring before their time—and all the more pleasing to the ear therefore.

22 MARCH: I took myself off to the marshes at twelve-thirty today, carrying Dreiser's editing of Thoreau's **Living Thoughts**, and walking slowly, so that I might take my fill of vesper sparrow and redwing song, of lark and killdeer singing, and the melodies of song sparrows and bluebirds. The water spiders were out on the brook, and I watched them briefly, and watched also a marsh harrier quartering the Lower Meadow. But presently I turned to Thoreau, and came almost at once upon his, "We can never have enough of nature." Indeed, it is so, I reflected immediately. But perhaps I had better say it is so also of me, for I am surrounded by nature at every possible moment, and yet have never enough of it, mosquitoes, reptiles, noxious weeds and vines notwithstanding. Moreover, I have come to think that no man is whole without a good deal of nature; certainly it is true that nothing is so soothing as nature, nothing so much a healer, not in her marvelous and beautiful softness, but in her implacable, inexorable, merciless sacrifice of life to perpetuate life, speaking in her thousand voices that out of earth all things have come, back to earth all things must go. It is sometimes a thing to marvel at that man is so content to be entertained by the cinema, the radio, the stage—anything to spare him the effort of using his muscles and his brain to investigate that greatest, most fundamental of all entertainments—the world around him, the world of which he is so infinitesimal a part. It is common enough to be stopped on the street and asked what manner of wild blossom I carry, but it is even more common to be asked what bloom I hold in hand when that bloom is no more than the pale yellow

blossom of the soft maple or the maroon-pink flower of the common elm, beneath which everyone in Sac Prairie must walk. Do they never lift their eyes to heaven, I wonder, or is it that they do indeed see clouds and sky, and nothing of what lies between? The trees are taken for granted—as shade, and shedders of leaves, and thus a source of unwelcome labor in autumn or early spring. It is inconceivable that millions of people live to old age without ever having seen the flower of the soft maple or the bloom of the elm, though these trees may have stood for decades in their own lawns, their pastures, along their fields and gardens and the streets of the village; and yet, unbelievable as it is, it is true; they miss the swelling buds, the flower, sometimes even the seed, and certainly they fail to see the delicate pastels of the spring leaves foretelling the autumnal colors. In like fashion, they know too little of the stars, of birds, of creatures and all things that grow, of insects; there are countless thousands for whom the face of heaven never changes, save for clouds; for them their knowledge of things that grow is limited to gardens, and encumbered by superstitions; of birds, they know only sparrows, grackles (which they call blackbirds), and jays, robins (which are destroyers of strawberries and cherries to them), crows, and hawks—like as not called eagles; of insects, they know the mosquito and the spider; and of fourfooted creatures, the gopher, the mole, rabbits, squirrels, raccoons—designed by God for the pleasure of their kind in shooting them. For them it will never be trite or worn to say with Thoreau, "We can never have enough of nature."

30 APRIL: Sitting in the dip atop the big hill this afternoon, with a strong east wind at my back, and the warm sun before, I could not work. Buttercups were yellow on the hill slope, and the everlasting was abloom today. Across the Wisconsin, the village glowed a pale soft green from trees breaking into leaf. I sat in the sun and contemplated time, how short it is, how no day is long enough for me, even in eighteen hours of wakefulness—and this is especially true in the spring, where time is very short, and the blossoms come and go before there has been time to enjoy each one adequately. The pasque flowers have hardly come to bloom before they are done; so, too, the hepaticas—now in blossom in the valley to northward—the dutchman's breeches, the anemones—which linger a little longer, true; the lilacs, the apple and plum and cherry bloom—in a moment, it seems, the long-awaited spring is gone, gone so much the swifter in proportion to the long period of anticipation. And with increasing years, inevitably, time passes more fleetly than ever before.

21 MAY: While estimating the numbers of birdfoot violets **(viola pedata)** and yellow-flowering vetch in my woodlot this morning, I saw what appeared to be a puff of smoke rising from among the dense trees northwest of the house, and hurried back to find not the fire I feared, but the scotch pine blooming, and singularly beautiful in flower: miniature two to three inch cones of flowers like tapers all over the tree in bright orange-yellow bloom. At every breath of air, at every puff of wind, a great cloud of pollen was swept away from the tree and dissipated among the red cedars and arbor vitae all around. While I stood looking at the tree, I was startled by the alarm signals of robins and lesser birds, and, following them to the larch along the outer fence, I was delighted to find one of my tenants: a mature beautifully proportioned specimen of the long-eared swamp owl—that nostalgic, melancholy cooing owl oft heard at evening and in the midnight dark. He surveyed me with an interest that equalled my own, bending forward a little with his ear tufts raised straight above his head, but presently flew from tree to tree back to the hemlock at the well, where he was well concealed, though not invisible, and where he still bent inquisitively forward to watch me. His actions indicated that his nest was not far away, which pleased me.

19 JULY: To the marshes at seven tonight, where I heard many bird calls, among them a seldom-heard field sparrow, singing as in spring. The liquid songs of wood thrushes held the evening air together with the lonely cries of pewees. In the Lower Meadow, hay had just recently been cut, and small green stacks of it stood in rows on the cutover area. Along the meadow a wonderfully fresh aroma held the air, rising from the sloughs on either side, and the massed foliage all around: a fall-like odor, cool and sweet. On the telegraph wires redwings swayed and sang and made a great to-do over their young, now all able to fly. Westward the sun was setting behind a low bank of thunderheads, rimmed on the upper edge with a deep, sullen coal-red color, vivid above the clouds' dark body.

3 OCTOBER: The song sparrows sang sweetly on the edge of night, and a white-throat gave forth his fluted Old Sam Peabody, Peabody, Peabody near the midmeadow slough. While I stood listening to him, the evening train went down, its great headlight and its clatter briefly silencing the birds, its green tail lights winking far down the tracks after it had gone, and its smoke holding to the evening like a pale fog upon the meadow to mingle with the mists rising along the brook.

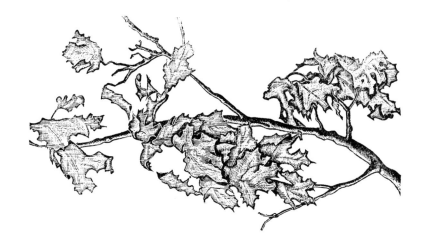

28 NOVEMBER: Entering into the eastern extremity of Wright's Valley in midafternoon today, I had not walked far before I was acutely conscious of the ineffable, pungent sweetness distilled from the frosted oak leaves—as if the frost draws from these dry, fallen leaves all the sweetness of summer, and there it lies in pockets and hollows among the hills, or rides the wind to be encountered anywhere —a perfume that carries in it so much of summer that the absence of autumn's early beauty has compensation here. This pungent aroma lay throughout the valley to the hill slopes along the river, where I paused to sit and look over the prairie; already the haze of early evening was beginning to show—a kind of luminous mist lying below the sun, and, immediately across the Wisconsin, the village was shadowed under faint wisps of smoke, the long shadows of houses making Sac Prairie to seem dark as in the early evening hours. No bird sang, no cloud held to the sky: a day of Indian Summer weather, and the scene before me here, encircled by the hills around that paw of land upon which the village lay, had in it autumn's essence with the warmth of summer, so that I was reluctant to leave the hillside to follow the old, familiar path back through the bottoms to Sac Prairie.

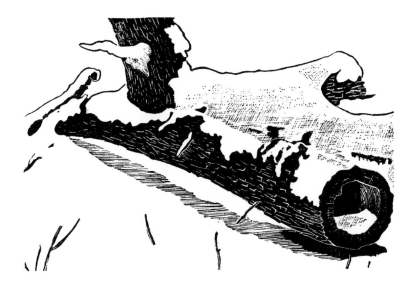

31 DECEMBER: The old hollow maple, for so long a place of refuge in sudden storm on the west edge of the Lower Meadow, is down at last.

THIS WOUND/1962

**Satellite**

As the satellite loomed among familiar stars,
adding its brilliance to Corvus, Pegasus, Andromeda,
drawing out of the north the aurora
flickering with unearthly beauty,
making its strange course through the heavens
to inform the night with wonder—

so you blazed across the landscape of the heart,
pervading each passing hour with delight,
quickening the pulse and the finite cells
of brain and bone
in the mysterious, unpredictable alchemy
of love.

**Absence**

A guitar troubles the moonlight,
speaking to me,
shatters the silence of evening
with warm, gentle notes—
as wind ripples the water,
glittering the dark—

a distant guitar
ruminant, pensive,
splinters the moonlight
as your absence splinters me.

## December Country

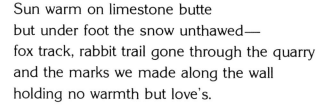

Sun warm on limestone butte
but under foot the snow unthawed—
fox track, rabbit trail gone through the quarry
and the marks we made along the wall
holding no warmth but love's.

Heaven blue, sun low, December's.

There is no need to speak.
We hold love humbly
beneath the towering wall,
before this soft, brown rolling land,
still and cold where no snow is,
no wind's rune, no bird's call,
and the wide, terrible stillness
is made bearable
only by love too tenuous to reach,
binding us each to each.

### The Sound of Silence

Standing in the deeps of moonlit woods, I heard
no wind's voice, no call of bird,
only the sound of silence
                    heard, heard,
in all the air, the moon-enchanted dark, the word
sung in the ear
            of silence ringing clear
in the moon's light, among the windless trees
and the shadows black on snow-bound
slopes of hill and swale of bottomland,
over the frozen ground and dark still water
flowing by:
            no voice, no sound, not heron's cry,
not wood-duck's cree, not hyla bell, not owl call
or whippoorwill:
            only the throbbing in the ear
like a distant tintinnabulation of far bells
echoing through the moonlit woods
from some strand farther than that moonlit shore
beyond the river where, turning in the midnight air,
are birth and death and all between.

Standing there
I heard, I heard—as the pulse secret within the
wintered bole,
as the waiting rill of March, as the heartbeat slow
in that hole cradling the sluggish frog—
I heard, I heard, as the turtle's muted pulse,
as the hidden flow of sap in buried root,
as the cry of love forbidden tongue, I heard
the sound rung clear—

and all once more was young,
begun again, turned newly to the earth and sky,
the amber eye of Mars, the Hunter's might, and Castor's
eye
caught in the bud-thick treetops where the sound swept by
to shatter on a footstep—the crunch of snow—
the whisper of one word—and if that word were love!

## Nocturne: Sugar Bush

There is a kind of day here,
not bright enough to see me by
except as spectral in the unclear
light of moon and stars come down the sky
to glitter in the thrusting branches
where the trees engage the moon
against the time of April's avalanches
of leaf and flower soon.

The maples, centuried with age,
yet green as in their first
green year, bleed into the cage
of buckets hung to slake the syrupmaker's thirst;
and I here among them half as old
bleed too in my own way,
of love once offered, now grown cold
and gone with age to grey—

while you, shadowed at the wood's edge dark,
stand indolently patient there to wait
upon my vagary to walk into this maple park,
dividing day from night, love from hate.

**Night Ride**

How quickly the road recedes,
the familiar landmarks—tree,
bush, signpost—blur, disappear!
and the mists rise to drown the valleys—
oh! and the moonlight in your eyes
lights up the willowisp I follow, follow
where time came and years gone by
fall and fade
along this midnight road.

Off the dark hill
a whippoorwill calls for my soul
as were it still my own to give.

**Parting**

When you pass from my sight
this lovely evening dies for me—
gone the enchantment of the sickle moon
and that one twilight star,
all lovers' planet. Only the owl cries
and the late hawk flies silently,
death in his talons—
and something in me too
is taloned by the little death
of parting
when dark and distance and the night
lie as time between forever.

COUNTRY PLACES/1965

## Owl: Midnight

Such as was once heard
pristine in wilderness,
unchanged: this dark-bound bird
comes upriver soundless
as late summer fog
brings close the barking
of a distant dog;

owl talk nearby,
across the meadow in the wood,
strong abroad under stars and sky—
where once deer stood
beneath this bough
I listen now.

I hear the deep tones
and the snapping beak.
I hear the primal wildness speak.

## The Light in the Haymow

Fire was the first thought that I had
when I saw that glowing bright
high in the gable—and then, a trick
of moonlight—but no: someone
    had left the light
burn in the haymow, and there it shone
something like a star
brought down close to the sweet hay
gathered and hauled in from far
afield—someone too busy to turn around
and look, to touch the switch
and give the mow to night
and time of owl and bat and witch-
fire—so there it shone as if
to illuminate, however, strange,
one man's motelike industry
against the universal range.

## Midnight Fox

Always by moonlight
and drifting cloud, the fox,
elusive, white-tipped brush
plumed behind, blackfooted legs
fleet, oh fleet where out of rocks,
out of cornrows, roadside,
out of the deep woods he goes
to ride the moonlight.

Always out of reach
of phantom hounds making music
as time somewhere at heels
baying, eyes of fire
burning bright
in the anonymity of night:
years telescope, time reels
where he goes by
indelible, sly.

Always the pulse leaps,
the heart quickens:
and I hasten, hasten
in the never-ending chase,
the cool pursuit
to match his race,
while the dark thickens
under cloud,
the moonlight hides
corn, mare's tails, fox spoor
where night rides
past, fast, fast
where one hour, one night
elusive fox and taut pursuer
will be last—
the same sheen of moonlight,
the same cloud shadow
always between . . .

## In the End Was His Beginning

Henry David Thoreau
July 12, 1817–May 6, 1862

The neighbors' children passed the house.
"Why don't they come to see me?" he said
to birdsong and the stirring of a mouse.
"I love them as if they were my own." He read
the morning star, the sunrise, the crying
of a meadow lark on the brightening edge of day.
Sam Staples said, "Never saw a man dying
with so much pleasure and peace." Time ticked
    on its way,
at Walden, at Fair Haven, and in the town
where his steps had scarcely ceased to stir the dust.
To that one who stood beside him looking down
and asked, "Have you made your peace with God?"
    he must
make such an answer as he did: "I did not know
that we had quarreled." And had he thought
about the other world? Light made show
in his reply: "One world at a time!" They ought
to have known him better after forty years—
surveyor of forest paths, bridges, dells and ravines,
inspector of snowstorms, student of wild careers
and hidden ways, knowing where the sassafras leans
upon the air, and the wild duck reared her young,
caretaker of beanrows and the bumblebee . . .
"I regret nothing," his words true on the tongue,
as the wind in the loneliest Concord tree.
The sun came. He spoke of moose
and Indians. At nine that May morning quietly,
    he died.
None knew his end was not yet to be. Children
    were loose
upon the town. Outside, a robin cried.

## On Hearing Church Bells in the Meadows

Far past the edge of the enclosing woods bells ring
to call the Sunday morning faithful in;
here nodding lilies grow, herons take wing
to forage all the ponds, and I, within
the sun on water and the meadow glow,
hear bells that ring alone for me
while warblers vault the blue in ecstasy
and phoebes drop to hunt mosquitoes low
above the water.

Such clarion calls ring here! Frog's cry,
birdsong, wind's hushing in the grasses,
leaves' murmur, white cloud in summer sky,
and the long memory of boyhood that never passes.
These bells ring for me above those
from that brick tower
summoning the faithful to worship for an hour;
here in this private Walden where April's seed
bursts forth, I worship according to my need.

## Maple Syrup Camp by Night

Inside all's warm and sugar sweet
where boiling sap above the fire
thickens—
but outside is crisp and clear
   with stars
among the budded maple branches.
Sparks course upward, under Arcturus,
red as Mars; my heart quickens,
leaps toward the looming Spring.

The sparks fly upward
and those up high wink out,
grow dark,
and I, left below,
stand inarticulate.

**Walking by Night in the Country**

The stars are down close to the trees,
the air crisp, no wind, no cricket or bird;
under these trees and stars and sky
only a dog heard,
and the rustling of dry leaves
where I go by.

Stars never more intimate,
the Great Dog leans on the hill
　　beside the road,
and the Hunter has climbed into
　　the leafless elm
to leaf it again with points of light
　　like stars.

Alone here and the clock stopped,
I am free among the stars.
The road leads from nowhere to nowhere
and the dog says all
that needs to be said.

WISCONSIN COUNTRY/1965

FOLLOWING LAST night's cold winter fog shrouding country and village, the white glory of hoar-frost clothed every house and shed, every bush and tree and roadside weed left free of snow; and for a few hours today the trees were white and singularly beautiful against the morning's blue sky, which seemed all the more blue in contrast. The village marshal, remembering how at one time he had worked in Argentine, Kansas, "a town on the Kaw," spoke of the recurrence of hoar-frost there —"Every night there was such a fog, and every morning that frost, even on the sidewalks, just like little icicles turned up."

There is nothing to compare with this most exquisitely wrought magic of the winter, though too many countrymen take such beauty for granted. I have never seen anyone examine one of the frost-bound boughs, never seen him enjoy the delicate patterns of the frost crystals; indeed, most passersby do not even look up, observing the hoar-frost as casually as they look upon the light of day and its mark upon a clock, walking under the frost-held trees as if they were reluctant to face into the heavens. Hoar-frost is but one of the multiple aspects of nature which offer unforgettable moments of beauty to all who will look. Perhaps it is that the concept of beauty has become rationalized into something static, something artificial or derivative, and the resultant blindness to the beauty of nature in every season can no longer be overcome except by long, enduring patience, which is too great a task for most men to undertake.

The hoar-frost this morning held for something more than two hours. I went walking along the country road toward the river, stopping now and then to take pleasure in closer scrutiny of the fragile patterns. At the Wisconsin's edge every branch, every weed, even the superstructure of the railroad bridge stood out in sparkling white against the dark blue water, every crystal of frost agleam in the morning sun, sending out millions of points of reflected sunlight, a kind of beauty all the more to be appreciated because of its rarity.

January

IN THE BOTTOMLANDS this afternoon, north of Hiney's Slough, I happened upon all that was left of the old hollow maple, once great enough to give shelter within its hollowed trunk to both Hugh and myself in our meanderings among the sloughs, since then blown down and lying prone, where for some time—two seasons—it budded and flowered and leafed out again, every twig of it, despite the tenuous connection it still had to earth. A few weeks ago it was budded and ready to flower and leaf again, but now Farmer Lenson has cut it up and carted most of its wood away. A part of its great hollow trunk still lay as it had fallen almost two years ago, but the tree would never leaf and blossom again; without its spreading branches, its ancient trunk would die. I saw that dry rot was evident well above the hollow place, so that in any event the tree could not have lived much longer; it was fitting that it should now go at last to feed fires to warm human beings, having lived close to two hundred years in uninterrupted majesty, host to bird and bee, enduring among red men and against the invasion of white men into its country, against the fires that swept the marshes year after year, against the incessant winds and the storms to which at last it fell. Nevertheless, I was saddened to see its proud branches cut, its budded twigs broken and chopped away to lie useless where once they had reared proudly skyward, towering high above the meadow and the blue water of the nearby slough; but it was perhaps the sadness which is natural in the face of change, an emotion to which all men are prey because change, like the clock's ceaseless ticking, is the face of time and the essence of life and the tangible reminder of death.

February

THE FIRST pussywillows showed catkins along the brook today. The grey looked out of split sheaths all along the stems there, standing lithe and immeasurably young among the osiers and alders, flaunting their announcement of spring despite the cold and snow all around. Their very presence seemed to diminish the cold of the wind blowing out of the west. Nor far away, in the soft ground at the slough's edge south of the trestle, the first green shoots of the aquatic plants there were in some places as much as three inches out of the earth, as bright to the eye in that place as the pussywillows were at the brook. Both were tangible reminders that even in the depths of winter, life goes on.

# March

IN THE BOTTOMS this evening not long after sundown, the season's first woodcock cried out, its nasal zeep, zeep rising from the groves of trees just south of the embankment along the east shore of Bergen's Island. At this hour the evening airmail was passing high over the southern tip of the islands, its lights winking red and green; along the western rim the afterglow pulled down, and the sickle of the new moon shone palely in the aquamarine above, and higher still gleamed the eye of Jupiter. The woodcock called persistently, and another voice was added to it, and yet another; indeed, soon the birds called from all sides, and in a little while the familiar mating flight, the aerial dance had begun, those awkward bodies hurtling darkly up into the darkling heaven in that ecstatic flight which has no equal for any countryman. I stood and watched one bird after another in its aerial dance, until the sky darkened and I could see no more; but I thought, as so often before, that there is a kind of uplift, an inspiring kinship, almost, in the watching of this rite.

WALKING THROUGH the park this evening, in a heaven of plum and cherry blossom perfume and the lilac fragrance rising from the bushes all around, I caught sight of the old Electric Theatre cornice above the buildings between the park and Water Street, and for one instant I was lost in time, I thought myself back in those early years when immediately after supper I had made my quick way to the theatre and there waited first for Bill Henning to open up, and then anxiously inside for Margery to come; and I reflected upon how often in the countryman's life—and doubtless in the life of anyone who remains within a familiar locality for any length of time—bridges to the clearest memory, however far in the past, are made in this fashion, by some small view not usually seen, or some small sound heard after a lapse of years, or a fragrance riding the wind—any one of which might bring back in the most minute detail the happening of which it was at one time an integral part. In a moment, the vision, the remembrance of time past, the sharp uncertainty of those years— all were gone; but for that isolated instant I had gone back almost two decades to early adolescence, I had experienced precisely the same high hope, tinged by anxiety and fear that something might keep Margery away; then the cornice was shut from view, the maples with their strong red new leaves and last buds rose between, and two decades made themselves manifest and proprietary once more.

May

WHILE HUNTING morels this afternoon I sat down in an old orchard to relax a little, and, while there, I heard suddenly the flicker-like frog note, the source of which I was not entirely certain. It rose from an old apple tree stump just behind me; so I got up and walked quietly over to it. The call emanated from a little hollow squarely on top of the old bole, but, peer as I might, I could not see him, so effective was his protective coloration. I poked gently about in the cavity with a stick and soon brought him into sight—a two-inch frog or so, with a granular grey skin mottled with darker grey or black, orange-yellow on the underside of the legs, large-eyed for his size, with the familiar extended ends of toes and fingers, and somewhat sticky on the underside—the common tree-frog, **hyla versicolor.** He struggled to get free; so I put him down into his hollow again, but he hopped back up, sitting on the edge of it and looking at me. I observed how perfectly his coat blended with the stripped, barkless grey of the old tree-trunk. After he had satisfied his curiosity, he retreated into the hollow once more, and presently began again to sing.

THE WILD strawberries were ripe on the slopes of the hills today, shining out of the grass in shady places. I stopped on the way to the Big Hill to pick and eat some of the succulent berries, which are always so much sweeter than domestic fruit, frightening up a robin which had been eating at that place. The robin attended my banquet with audible sounds of mourning, as if I were about to end his repast, but he returned to his own board as soon as I took my departure.

THE MEADOWS and roadsides were radiant with blossoms today—lavender Joe-Pye weed, mauve ground-nut, penstemons, ironweed, many varieties of sunflowers, spotted touch-me-not, the beautiful taper-like spires of wild balsam apple or wild cucumber, white boneset, turtle-heads or balmony, and many more flowers, lending to the meadows not only the colors of yellow and lavender so common to late summer or early autumn, but also effecting a kind of haze lying just above the grasses, so that it was as if an extension of color there.

THE HILLS this afternoon were a glory of white daisies. I could not remember ever having seen so many of them; slope upon slope were white with waist-high daisies standing tall over all other blossoms—of vervain, bergamotte, primroses, St. John's wort, ox-eye daisies, ironweed, peppermint, yarrow, clovers, penstemons, and even most mullein.

NIGHTHAWKS mounted heaven and coasted down the sky this evening over the low hills along the Mazomanie road, just across from the Spring Slough trestle, where I stood to watch how they spiralled aloft, erratically, making their nasal, twanging peent, peent, and then, at the height of their upward flight, closing their wings and plummeting downward, only to swing sharply upward not far above the trees, with the wind in their suddenly stiffened wings sounding a resonant zoom. The four or five birds which were aloft when first I noticed them soon lessened in number; most of them began to fly westward, toward the Wisconsin, to forage for insects in flight over the water there, leaving three and two, and finally but one bird, but this one flew for a long time, crying up heaven and coasting down, a dark, diminishing object on the darkening heaven, and was lost at last in the deepening twilight.

# October

AFTER READING throughout the afternoon, I watched the swift changes in the approaching dusk from the head of the Big Hill. The sun was low, just above the line of the Ferry Bluff range in the southwest, perhaps twelve degrees above the rim of earth in a yellow glory there on the upper edge of that typical autumnal haze which is so much a part of October days in Wisconsin. The western hills had darkened; occasional beams of sunlight slanted still to the slopes that curved northward along the northwest hills, gleaming from brilliant patches of foliage, from the ventilators on the barns along the base of the foothills before the Baraboo bluffs. The slopes of the tall bluffs in the north, above the broad cobalt line of the river, still held the sun and lay warm there, but already a touch of evening's blue had come into the red haze imparted by the groves of claret and maroon oaks. To eastward, the immediacy of Breunig's hill and its twin to the north made their slopes bright still with sunlight, though where I sat the shadows were already long, and the earth a pale rose in color. Birch and oak were bright on the immediate slopes, ranging in color from bright yellow, chrome, ochre, and dull copper to cardinal, crimson, claret, magenta, maroon cerise, saffron, old rose, vermilion, mauve, sienna, and leather-brown. Sac Prairie itself lay in a kind of blue-red haze, the blue smoke rising from a score of leaf-fires burning along the gutters and in the alleys; it was dark with the shadows of its still well-leafed trees, so that sunlight shone only from an occasional side wall or a window among the trees, mellow and old there among the houses, though the river's shore along the west was already held in the first shadow of twilight. As the sun went down, the shadows drew in both from east and west—from the east as the light drew away, from the west as the tall shadows of the hills reached across the prairie to the village; soon only the red ball of the sun shone in the west, and a pale effulgence on the brightly-leafed slopes to the east, and then dusk deepened on the earth.

# November

WITCH-HAZEL blossomed along the Otter Creek where it flowed through Baxter's Hollow at the upper edge of the prairie today, standing in yellow glory in the dark hollow, with its thin, wiry petals fully open, making a yellow haze along the barren branches: that strange bush, leafless, yet flowered now in this season of seed and fruit, used by water diviners and wizards in time gone by. Its haze of blossoms vied along the creek there with the small red berries of wintergreen. Wherever it grew, it stood in small, compact groves, making a kind of light of its own all the more startling for the sombre darkness of the hollow all around.

December

AT THE SECOND Brook trestle Hugh went down the embankment and plucked a silkweed bloom, and both of us paused to appreciate the singular beauty of the individual blossoms of this composite, and to smell the delicate fragrance of the flower, doubly strong tonight because of the air's moisture after rain. The richness of this common milkweed is too little known, and its carnation-like perfume often passed by, like too many things simply taken for granted, save in the autumn, when its silk tempts passing children to assist nature by scattering the brown tufted seeds in the wind.

THE ONLY PLACE WE LIVE/1966

**Letter**

Between the lines of your letter
this morning I read more
than you may have said—
or meant to say

and all this afternoon in the lowlands
where I walked, birds' cries
and the wind's rune in leafless branches
put into words for my ear alone
what you said between the lines—

and every tree and stick
and stone had a new brightness
of which the source was love.

## By Owl Light

Deer in the cornstubble—
on the western rim the umbral moon
going, going,
and across, on the dark east,
the eye of spring where
Arcturus looks into the frosty air.

The deer see me
and I hear the sounds they make
in the dry stubble where they go
far downfield between the winter moon
and the ploughman's star.

I am alone here in the wan dark
caught in the February night
as in the hollow of your hand,
loosing the spring again in me.

## Sugar Bush Afternoon

Something is going on here below
unhinted in the wind's rune high above,
something in a thousand drops, slow, slow,
with a tin sound or a water sound.
The blue sky is far overhead and one cloud
foretelling another little winter.
The sap flows sweet from the maples
in the sugar bush
and the snow scarce thawed
where our footprints were, yours and mine.
Your voice echoes near in the sound
of the drops into the pails ringing
the trees, but the wind carries it away,
carries me from yesterday into today,
and the lashing branches, the wet ground,
the quickened pulse all make the signature
of spring.

Forgive me my disloyalty—
I hear the heartbeat of each tree
louder than my own,
and the hushing wind speaks of more
here than love
(as were there more),
tearing the cries from the throats of crows
passing by, tearing your name
from my lips and heart,
scattering the sound among a thousand,
thousand drops of life
spilling from the spiles.

## Roses at the Roadside

Old roses linger long where once
a home stood at the roadside,
giving their fragrance to the summer air—
Harrison's yellow and old-fashioned red
abide with fox-tail grass and elderberry,
and the long-abandoned house,
offering nocturnal haven to owl
and whippoorwill, is less than a shell
on the side of the hill,
like the husk of love gone by
with its memories lingering—
old roses unwilling to die.

BY OWL LIGHT/1967

**April**

April is that month
    leaves unfold
    and gardeners
    quicken
that month
    squills
    crocuses
    tulips
    hyacinths
        bloom
and on the hills
    pasque flowers
    open their pale blue eyes
    wild
    for wind and sun
that month
    of woodcocks mating
    and frogs celebrating
    love . .
April is that month
    the heart
    renews itself.

## Grackles

Suddenly one morning the grackles blacken
the trees, and all day talk and sing—
trees almost leafless, fern and bracken
brown, and the wind blowing up to bring
the cold.
      The grackles warm the hours
with their intimate chatter and to-do.
A low bank of cloud along the west lours
and threatens rain, belying the high blue
over.
    The grackles spin a soft cocoon
enclosing trees and field, and all
within earshot throughout morning, afternoon—
winter is far away, just beyond the garden wall.

What talk they make of places
far and near where they have been,
fluttering wings and turning bronze faces
sunward! The light makes a sheen
upon their glossy coats.
    All day this talk of distant places,
from sunrise to the sickle moon, and then
their silence making poignant knowledge
of how short man's race is,
how little a world is that of man!

## Night Traveler

Come from his hollow tree beneath the moon,
he scatters fallen leaves where he walks
in leisure through the dark, an inquisitive raccoon
exploring brush and pool and the leaning stalks
of reeds.
      He goes along the moonlit sloughs
to dip his paws for crayfish; frogs go fast
beyond his reach. Tree and forest floor and pond
    all wear the hues
of iridescence where moonlight falls and last
of day is gone. Lover of night, the old raccoon
goes rustling up and down, in search of food;
he drinks the leaf-sweet air, and celebrates the moon;
he fills the evening with his mood.

His footsteps fall loudly to the listening ear;
to one going by close enough to hear,
these footfalls open up a world apart from light,
and add a new dimension to the night.

### Owl Before Dawn

The owl that ruminates before the dawn
bells the dark, and I hear him going on
long before the lark at this hour
of echoing silence on the waning edge
of night.
      We carry on a kind
of dialogue, he and I, except for that
I do not speak. No matter. Reply
is there deep inside, soundless,
in this dialogue of life and death.

How persuasively he speaks!
I lie awake this early hour—or late,
and listen, listen. How many answers
to life's questions are explicit
in the dark!

### A Little Elegy for My Father

William J. Derleth
1883-1965

The echo of his whistling at work
stalks the rooms of this house he built,
like a ghost never to be laid.

How he loved the feel of wood
in his hands! He built to last.
Strange in this house he wrought
with such capable hands
to think of him as past.

He who was yesterday is gone today:
what he left stands.
He loved work; he must be doing,
shaping, building, repairing,
with the same hands that now and then held
a small boy's fishpole, patient with his son
impatient for Wisconsin sunfish,
bluegills—strong wandering the hills
for butternuts, hickorynuts, wild cherries.

I hear his whistle echo still, bell-clear.
Oak and pine give it back, with
a tantalizing hint of smoke from his cigar.
In all he did love was understood,
as tangible as wind's rune in the aspen tree,
the saw's song cutting through the wood
against his knee.

"We listen to the dead.
We are sure they will not deceive us . . .
with words unbiased by greed, love, anger."

I listen, Father.
I listen, listen, and I hear
the echo of that whistling joy
in work, sweetening life
for man and boy. I listen, Father. Speak,
who said enough in happiness at work
to make the lesson clear.

WALDEN POND/1968

THE SLOPES of the hills around the pond were heavily wooded still, even as they must have been when Thoreau, living here, heard the eternal pulse of infinity in the voices of his wild neighbors. There were drying sweet-ferns along the path as well, the narrow, regularly toothed leaves beginning to curl and brown a little and too dry to give off their fragrance, but the pungence of pines held to the air in this dry season—there did not appear to have been any rain of consequence for some time, but the soil would readily have absorbed rain, and traces of it would soon be lost, except in a very wet time of the year.

TURNING OVER his words in this place where, conceivably, they had taken shape for him, I was made to think of Sac Prairie, where, I suppose, I engage life in somewhat similar circumstances, allowing for a century's advance in time and that signal difference between an older New England village like Concord and a comparatively young Midwestern settlement like Sac Prairie, neither being exactly typical of its milieu. I could not deny certain parallels, quite apart from a unanimity of thought and an agreement in conclusions. Thoreau made pencils; I publish books, apart from writing for other publishers, as did he. Though there is no pond of Walden's size at my doorstep, the Wisconsin river flows down to the village out of the north and curves around it to the west, with its backwaters and sloughs, and the brooks that feed into it—not, perhaps, as intimate a stream, being broader, as the Concord or the Sudbury or the Assabet, but one that nevertheless makes its presence widely known in the village, and draws to itself the same breed of fishermen and trappers that were drawn to the rivers of Concord more than a century ago.

There are still solitary places in the woods and the marshes around Sac Prairie where, as Thoreau found it at Walden, only a railroad can be seen to remind one of civilization—where pewees and hermit thrushes and veerys sing—where the prints of deer and mink, of raccoon and fox and opossum and even, rarely, wildcat can be seen; places where it is possible to come face to face with one's self, without the intrusions of living patterns and mores imposed by others, where nature is all and the wisdom of the wind and the soil, in frog song and bird cry, in the always visible pattern of life and death impels a man's private accounting. But there cannot be much summer solitude at Walden today, to judge by the wearing away of the path . . . .

Each of us makes his accommodations with life, as Thoreau did. Each adjusts to circumstances when he cannot be their author. Each comes to terms with existence, though the terms differ widely, and the compromises some men make are frequently denigrating and defeating. For every man who finds his private Walden, there are many thousands who never know a refuge, whose existence is mere resignation, who never learn that the universe is wider than their view of it. To Thoreau his Walden, to me Sac Prairie—a sort of Walden West, in which I have traveled no less widely than Thoreau at Concord, and in which I am involved as much as if not more than he in his village, each taking time to explore his private seas, as well as to improve his acquaintance with the setting and its inhabitants, learning what goes on not only in the woods but also in the hearts of men.

As I sat there, lines from **Walden** came readily to mind. The setting gave them immediacy, and the reflections they induced were such as to emphasize certain parallels between Thoreau's way of life and mine. It was manifestly easier, by contrast with the mid-twentieth century, to lead so independent an existence as Thoreau led, for there were Waldens at every hand. The world was not much with Thoreau, for it did not press in upon him; today he would meet it full wherever he turned and would be appaled at its savage materialism. In another century the very slopes of Walden may be covered with houses pressing close one upon another.

A SOMBRE note persisted at thought of the world outside, a world Thoreau himself had not fully anticipated, one in which the compulsion toward wealth and material comfort helped to bring about the destruction of much that Thoreau loved; one in which large areas of the countryside were being drenched with pesticides that destroy or sterilize birds by the millions, while the insects they were meant to eliminate are rapidly developing ever more effective immunities, which the birds, slower to evolve, could not do in time to prevent their eventual extermination; a world in which little men who have no concept of beauty destroy the road-sides to encourage speed, and cover large parts of the landscape with concrete instead of grass; a world in which the human animal—who alone among animals habitually befouls his environment —has elevated the technology of destruction to a plane high above the level of creation, so that he invariably destroys, in peace as well as in war, far more than he creates. A world, in short, in which millions of people, young and old, but most espe-cially the young, know little or nothing of nature beyond that part of which they learn from books or view in a zoo, in which men and women who appreciate natural beauty and the simplicity of life close to the earth and in kinship with other, non-human earth-dwellers, are in an ever-narrowing minority.

CAITLIN/1969

### Dandelion

One dandelion you asked—
That modest flower
though yellow is the color
of the sun, the moon,
of gold and goldenrod,
of daisies
and of pride . . .

Nevertheless,
considering the complex
ramifications of love,
I offer it to you,
Caitlin—
but color it red
with my heart's blood.

## Wild Geese

The cries of wild geese passing by
woke me to the dark, and I rose
to the window to look in vain
for that skein under the starlit sky.
Outside, the spectral bough,
and silence broken only by the call
of one far owl and the fading now
of honking down the night.

I could not go back
to that bright dream of love,
my bed too lonely without you,
so walked the dark from wall to wall
beneath that same vast sky.

What was your dream this night?
And did you hear the migrant hosts
ring out their freedom going by?

Oh, Lady, how dark it is here
with all these ghosts!

**Graffiti**

The world is innocent.
It is we who are not.
The wind knows no moral,
the sun brightens the sands
of the seashore free
of any philosophy,
the worm waits
without ethical considerations
on this avid flesh to rot.

The world demands
our connivance at the erosion
of its innocence.

THE LANDSCAPE OF THE HEART/1970

## Upstate Village: Summer 1968

What I thought
was smoke
of sycamore leaves
was toadflax
hot in the sun.

I stood bemused
by it
when I ought
to have looked down
through the hot
shimmering air
and seen how
somewhere, somewhere
in this town
—not far, not far—
you waited
for me to see
how beautiful you are.

On the willows
pearled with catkins
the redwings (**Agelaius phoeniceus** . . .
in temperate zones an early
spring arrival . . .)
swing, and in their joy
sing conqueree,
conqueree . . .

## The Green Season

Killdeers (**Charadrius vociferus** . . .
sometimes the first bird
to reach Wisconsin in March . . .)
fly wild, wild,
low over field and hill
and cry, cry, spill
nostalgia . . .

Out of the bog,
waiting on the hyla,
on the first frog,
a song sparrow (**Melospiza melodia** . . .
sometimes a winter staybehind—
trills its threnodies . . .)

and Caitlin,
in me the hot blood
pulses with what
has no season
and yet's eternal spring—
sings love,
love . . .

**April Morning**

This rain-washed, sap-flowing
morning is fresh
as first love,
and where I walk
listening to flicker cry
and jacksnipe winnowing
and the talk of ducks in the slough,
I think of you, Lady,
with love, naturally,
and passion.

On such a morning,
with the first flowers
opening in the maple trees,
it does not matter
how naked we are
to our enemies.

**Whippoorwill**

Caitlin,
we are not alone
in this owl-flight time
under the spill of moon,
not alone in a world
not our own
where the dark hill looms—
but that bird out there
crying whippoorwill
shares the ache
and the longing . . .

His red eye glows
like a jewel
in headlight shine
at the edge of the road
and shows him
as day's light
reveals us
each to each
and to the world's
greedy reach.

**Graffito**

In this meadow the vast
impersonal expanse of snow,
the call of one crow far
down the strand,
an abandoned cart
under the dome of sky—
and the cry in my heart
to you, are all the world . . .

Lady, it is only
when we love
that we understand
how alone we are.

RETURN TO WALDEN WEST/1970

WE SELDOM did anything memorable at the hill-top farm—we hunted birds' nests, combed the open woods for wild strawberries and, later, black-capped raspberries, we went either to the Crary or John Ring houses to play or forage, we walked through the woods, played games, especially hide-and-seek, enjoyed the hay stored in the barn—all the trivial events to which children isolated on a farm, too far from town, were given.

Sometimes, on still, hot days, the farm drowned in the musk of animals and the barnyard, but there was usually some movement of air on the hilltop, particularly at night, so that mosquitoes and gnats were never much of a problem, and the nighthawks and whippoorwills and bats that darted and swooped there after insects could not have had very good hunting, save at the woods' edge, where the wind did not disperse the insects.

The little storey-and-a-half house hardly accom-modated us all, but we were in and out all day long, and we were never conscious of being crowded, though some of us had to sleep on the floor.

THE HOUSE wore its informality well. It invited one in and those who lived there never betrayed the atmosphere of the old house—for the house was old, closer to a hundred years in age than to fifty when first I knew it—and it never disappointed me, whether I came upon Emmy looking through an old photograph album or whether I walked in upon the Christmas Eve party, when the house was at its warmest and most cheerful, with its brightly-lit tree and the long table around which we all sat remembering older years and older inhabitants who had gone before, recounting lives and anecdotes before the little gathering—seldom more than twenty people—broke up in time for midnight mass at St. Aloysius. It was the kind of house one was impelled to visit for none but the most casual reasons—for small talk, or a game of bridge, for it was a house that drew more aimless cousins like Meta Meyer, who cheerfully took part in two or a dozen games of bridge while chattering about the events of her life, those events that loomed so large to her and were in reality so pitifully small, so that one could never tell who might be there in addition to the regular inhabitants.

HUGO WAS, particularly because of his silence, the ideal hiking companion, for it was never necessary to convey in words the sight of a rare bird or the hearing of a wilderness voice what a glance at each other could say well without interruption of the natural sounds of the wild.

IN WARM April evenings, the toads begin to sing along the Wisconsin, in the meadows and sloughs, in the marshes, the indigenous toad in the Sac Prairie area being **Bufo Americanus**, commonest of his species. Their pleasant, lulling trill falls so melodically to the ear that it is difficult to realize that a song of such liquid clarity and beauty could come from a creature so unlovely to look upon as a toad, as if the song were compensation for its warty skin and basilisk eyes.

No other nocturnal song quite matches it; the toads' steady trilling striking several, varied keys makes a choir that is an auditory delight not duplicated by nature in Wisconsin. They will not give voice in song until both warmth and humidity reach a desired level, never reached until April, and sometimes not until May; but once begun, the toads' songs can be heard throughout the night, throughout the spring, well through the summer, though a subtle change gradually comes over the song, a change in tone and tempo.

Toads' trilling makes a steady background of pleasant sound for songs and cries of birds and other batrachians celebrating the spring in the hot afternoons, the sultry evenings. The singing has a quality of peace and contentment, of continuity; however urgent it may be to the singers, it carries calm and temperance to the solitary walker in the night, imparting its contentment even as, by night, the whippoorwill spreads its loneliness and haunting nostalgia.

In spring, the song is companioned by many voices; in the summer nights it vies with tree frogs and wood ducks in the same milieu; the songs and cries blend, coming in out of the dark, but it is the toads' trilling that lasts and lingers to assure the solitary walker that the life of the pond and the bottomlands is constant and eternal.

A HOST OF sounds, scarcely audible or so seldom repeated as to go all too often unheard, companion the well-known voices of the night—the low, cooing hoot of a long-eared swamp owl, the muted conversation of teal, the bell-like song of the saw-whet owl—existing on the very rim of awareness. Who, among the most solitary of night-walkers, commonly hears the quirting of whippoorwills, the mewing talk of muskrats, the voices of voles and meadow mice? Yet these sounds are everywhere in the spring and summer evenings, lost among the more commanding songs of birds and frogs, or so subdued as to be audible only to the waiting ear.

There are, too, the occasional unidentifiable sounds, the strange voices of uncommon birds or animals—of a migrant bird not native to the Sac Prairie country, stopping briefly overnight, or an animal long alien to this place passing through under cover of darkness, or the infinite small variations in the songs of little known warblers or frogs lend a tantalizing strangeness to evening and night, rising out of the dusk and darkness of the woods and announcing that briefly an unknown visitor has paused in this familiar milieu, and will be gone again ere the inquiring eye can find him —of a bird little given to voice, like the black-crowned night heron whose barbaric cry rises now and then out of the slopes near the river. Such voices invest the night with something alien, but are not apart from the dark wood itself, for was not a dark wood forever the heart of mystery, the source of the unknown from the beginning of man's consciousness?—since it stood for the tangible foe of man as he conceived it: earth itself arrayed against his small fire and multitude of his fears.

The night speaks with many voices in the thousand tongues of earth, not all known to the listening ear; each shouts its triumph in life into the enclosing womb of darkness, under the moons and stars and suns of this one infinitesimal galaxy in the cosmos; each throbs in harmony with the pulse of the night-walker passing by, of whom the habitants of the dark and darkening wood are often less aware than he of them. He may not know whence these voices come; he might be astonished to discover that the fluted piping making a choir of an April night in the meadows rises from a creature so small as to take three or four of them to cover the face of his watch; that the least breath of sound may come from the sleek, magnificent otter, a creature of size and power; that the ventriloquial voice of a screech owl rises not from many yards away but almost at his elbow; that the wild, sobbing scream from the high hills is the voice of the now rare wildcat.

The night is filled with voices—the sounds of gnawing, the songs of mating, the scuttering of passage, the screams of death, constantly, forever, the step of the night-walking solitary marking off another moment of his allotted time before he returns to dust which he will share in common with all the known and unknown habitants of the wood around him, all in due, inexorable time; the hyla choir no less than the whippoorwill's song, the jack-snipe's weird winnowing no less than the wild duck's whistling, the rabbit's death scream no less than the beaver's insatiable gnawing, the rustling of mice passing by no less than the weasel's remorseless pursuit, the love song of the woodcock no less than the proud high cry of the hunting hawk are all integral to the pattern of life and death.

THE WINTER marshes drew me on temperate days of thaw. I went in along the brook from the Mazomanie road, crossed the Brook Trestle, and followed the brook bank to the ash-grown place where it emptied into the east channel of the Wisconsin. The path I took was open to the meadow on the south and walled off on the north by woods and underbrush on the far side of the brook, a woods thick enough to hold off the north wind and leave the meadow side of the brook warm with pooled sunlight.

All along the brook rose the subdued voices of the meadows—the whispered songs of tree sparrows and juncos, the cries of tufted titmice, the phe-be-be of chickadees, the warnings of blue jays, the occasional threnody of a song sparrow that elected to remain for the winter, the melodies of purple finches, the complaints of robins which, too, chose not to migrate and made a small flock of birds that fed on the berries and seeds so plentiful in the lowlands, vying for food with the mice and voles that climbed the reeds for seeds, and left tracks in the snow that told of urgent need and sometimes—in spots of blood, fox tracks that ended in pouncing marks, or the print of owl's wings—of sudden death.

Across the meadow crow caws rang out in the crisp winter air and echoed against the bills that rose into the eastern sky beyond the meadow and the Milwaukee Road spur that bounded it on that side, while from the woods rose now and then the scream of a red-shouldered hawk, an eruption of calls from a group of barred owls, the high, challenging notes of a pileated woodpecker, the drumming of a grouse, a rare gyrfalcon's cry or a kingfisher's rattle where he flashed along the brook.

Sunlight lay mellow on the snow-covered meadow, coming out of the low southern sky, gleaming from blades of grasses that stood above the snow, and heightening the color that abounded all winter long in the lowlands—the red osier wands, the mustard willows, the maroon of soft maple buds that arbored the path beside the brook—and the fruit on which the smaller birds fed: orange bittersweet, the brown, beautifully sculptured climbing false buckwheat seeds, the clustered dark blue carrion berries, the cerise fruit of the burning bush or wahoo, the coral berries ranged thickly on the twigs of the black alder and shining out of the dark woods even at a distance like pale red torches, sweetbriar's dark blue fruit, and the red rose haws that stood in many places, in and along the meadow. Great old maple trees grew on the western rim of the meadow out of a swale there; beyond them the brook meandered through a region orange with a thick growth of bittersweet twining among the prickly ash, and, under an old black ash, opened into the river.

I became accustomed to sitting at the sunlit base of the most open of the maples, facing south, to read and write, far removed from my fellowmen, occasionally startling a deer or a passing hawk, jeered at by crows, with the meadow unraveling to the south and the distant woods there, and at my right the trees crowded between the meadow and the river, while to the east the meadow reached to an old haybarn there, beyond which the tall, snow-clad hills lay on the sky like frozen thunder; and, tiring of this place went up along the drainage ditch that divided the meadow there to sit at the south wall of the old barn, which on a day of thaw gave off all the fragrance of June in the perfume of the hay that came out between the warped, old unpainted boards of its walls. I spent many winter hours there, sitting on a spill of hay left behind by the farmer who came now and then throughout the winter to haul away a load of the summer marsh's yield, taking the sun, writing—principally poems, none of any great merit, however pleasing they seemed to eye and ear.

The brookside path and the adjacent meadow were places of singular tranquility—a domain of mouse and crow, rabbit and fox, of vole and shrew and hawk—tranquility that the passing train not only did nothing to disturb but actually seemed to enhance, winding its way along the tracks from the south and through the woods over the Spring Slough Trestle on the way into Sac Prairie like a great beast with box-cars and caboose colored red and green, yellow and orange, chuffing past and rattling through that lowland like any inhabitant of the country, its whistle echoing flatly over the meadows like the distant lowing of cattle at the Lenson farm along the highway east.

Here on some day in late winter, while snow still patched the earth, the first spring voice would sound—a killdeer's wild kildee, kildee, where the bird flew in low over the meadow out of the south—a redwing's conqueree, rising from the meadow's edge along the railroad embankment, where that black, glossy bird with its bright shoulder patch swayed on a catkin-pearled willow—the shrill ee-ee of a marsh harrier—the high cry of an osprey, now but rarely seen—the chortling song of a bluebird flying over—the mimetic sounds of starlings; and along the brook muskrat and mink and beaver would once again set about the business of living, while high in the blue the wild geese would fly over in great arrows and wedges, honking their way north; and the meadow would soften and the brook overflow to shut away the meadows from me until summer firmed the earth once more, the water returned to within its banks, and I to the hills.

I NEVER found that nature failed me in the continuity of time and place so necessary to my well-being. While the condition of man on his planet slowly worsens, the pattern of the seasons changes not at all, however much nature's aspects reflect the damage wrought by man in his avarice and his devotion to false, unnatural values.

After every winter, there comes a day when the first frog begins to sing, when the first killdeer's nostalgic cry rings out over the still snow-patched meadows, when the vanguard of the redwings sing from the willows and the first threnodies of the year's first song sparrow rise from the brook-side, the wild geese go honking over into the north, and the caroling of robins and the keening of mourning doves fill the village evenings between sundown and dark, when the catkins pearl the willows and aspens. The sere, snowcovered earth gives way to green, the green makes place for the deep yellow of buttercups and cowslips, the blue of squills, pasque-flowers, irises and violets, and leaves spill their subtle musk into the sunny afternoons, and life burgeons again.

In the village as in the country, birth and death know no winter; here life is more patently unceasing change. Familiar faces vanish, long-known voices sound no more, gone to ground. The young grow up to confront a life ever more complex, and in their time are harried to the grave, scores of men and women who may never see the beauty of the earth they live in, who may never know themselves as integral to nature.

I walk among them, it often seems, increasingly an alien, informed by compassion and understanding, but less content among my fellow men than in the marshes or the hills, on the river or along a country road at night, where I am closer to coming full circle, to awareness of that ultimate darkness that is the merging of the self with time and the inevitable dust.

## Apologia

LONG AGO, during the years of my childhood, I was lost forever to the world in which men engaged life in momentous concerns and affairs, charmed away by the world intimately near to my senses

—of sunlight dappling a pond, the voice of running water, the matins of robins and mourning doves, the pensive threnodies of pewees and song sparrows, the majestic beauty of hawks aloft, the breathlessly exciting dance of woodcocks in the chill spring evenings, the shyness of violets and hepaticas, the arrogance of crows

—bewitched by the song of the hermit thrush and veery, by the wild nostalgia of killdeers and whip-poorwills, by meadows yellow with cowslips or dusty rose with Joe-Pye weed, by hylas in April song and by fireflies in June, by the keening of screech owls in the night, by the lulling songs of toads in the spring ponds

—captivated by the wind's runes and the river's moods, by dewhung grasses, lilacs and columbines, by the redwing's early conqueree, by pussywillows and maple musk, by wild plum bloom crowding the woods' edges and the line-fences, by sunset and afterglow, new moon and evening star, by cloud and tree and hills, by pasture rose and coronilla, by rain and snow and nighthawks coasting down the buttes of sky, by wild geese aloft, by mosses and mushrooms in field and forest

—and the solitudes of men and women who lived in this same world, as intimately near as I, and saw it seldom or never at all

—and all I did thereafter was done to enable me to live out that special enchantment and explore that world where the major concerns of other men did not matter—not fame or wealth or the pursuit of other phantoms conjured up by hope or love, valor or avarice.

# The Only Place
# We Live

JESSEStuart

The blackbirds and the geese are going south
The grass has died before its time to die.
The grass has browned and purpled from the drouth
And copper clouds are ledged upon the sky.
The ground-hogs bury in their winter holes
Squirrels are nesting in the hollow trees
The blind black snake hunts for a winter hole.

Out of the wintry past I still remember
The day I drove my truck into the wood
In filigreed, clean frost of late November,
I saw a thing almost chilled my blood.
Turning a log embedded in the ground
Where there was roof and wall against the cold,
My setter's sniffling so quickly found
A pretty, parent, baby-handed mole.
There in her nest he crushed her instantly,
But not the babies suckling at her breast,
Whose small eyes were still closed in infancy
And bodies were exposed to winter's blast,
This scene remains embedded in my brain:
I took four naked young from their dead mother
Into my home against the sleet and rain
And raised them on goat's milk with an eyedropper.

It is too late for beetles now to sing,
Too late for butterflies to drink from flowers
In these brown autumn leafstrewn woods of ours.
This is the time of frost
And wild bird cries;
The time of ripe leaves
And blue windy skies.

I love recesses by cool autumn streams
Where wild grass is the color of my skin
And secret places of the earth are home.

I choose this night and know the path to take
Through sumacs, red oaks, winding like a snake.
My blood runs wild but wilder is my mood
I'm free to listen to the music flood.
My blood runs up like warm sap in a tree
I run on paths where foxes ought to be.

There are delights in living close the earth
I know — for I have lived 'neath roots of trees
I feel the heartbeats of the earth deep under
Our brains are sensitive to loud spring thunder.

Sing out, sing out, you lonesome waters, sing!
Sing to the drooping fern, the tendril shoots;
Sing to the bright clean wind,
For this is spring.

Magnificent this world where each partakes
Of breathing cool clean unpolluted air
Attached to time and place in his review
Of his small world where days have been the same
Day after day in his yesteryears.

I have gone down at midnight — sat beside you
Your lonesome bankside trees — your pulsing will
Was surging your body down one last way
Like some deep singer in the void you fling
Futility to the wind and flow and sing
While I return to where my candle flame
Burns low and the world will never know my name.

I'm thankful for a wife who will arise
And go with me before the birds awake
While morning darkness still is in our eyes
To help me with the work I undertake
To go afield before the light of morn.

The otter chooses silver fish for nurture
Delicate morsel for an otter's taste
The otter only satisfies the hunger
Unlike our species who will kill to waste.

Darkness is settling around the woods in
Less than one hour night will be falling here.
For now the shadows lengthen on the ground
And it is time we should be leaving here.

I have heard mean groans of heavy engines
Striking the emptiness of night
And I have heard the drive wheels slipping
When the track was sanded.
I have heard the lonesome whistle screaming
I have heard the oozing steam from slick pistons
The swinging and banging of boxcar doors
The sounds I have loved.

I shall not go inside the church tonight
She must not see me stagger down the aisle
She must not be ashamed of me tonight
Church will be over in a little while.

My mother said Liz Reeder's baby died.
It lived ten minutes after it was born.
The doctor could not come, or else he lied
Knowing she was heavy with Bill's child.

She will not see the sun tomorrow rise,
Nor see tomorrow's evening sun go down;
For cankered pennies will lie on her eyes
And she will sleep in her best dressing gown.
Her twelfth babe will be pillowed on her arm,
Her living will look at her sleeping face;
They will remember how she had feared harm
For them if she should find a resting place.
Will there be one to keep a roof for them,
To mend their clothes and bring them food to eat?
And when they go beyond the ridge's rim
Who'll counsel her young daughters of deceit?
Her young sons of hypocrisies and snares?
How can she rest in peace with only one
When she has left eleven living cares?
She cannot sleep from death to morning sun.

I want to leave these hills I've known since birth
For they are things I have grown to despise.
I shall not miss our neighbors and our mules;
I shall not miss our cattle, fields and trees;
I shall not miss my home, my folks, farm tools
I've been a wounded dreamer since my birth.

The destiny of man is big, my friend,
As high as walls of blowing wind are high;
There is no end to love and joy and kiss,
No end to all the futile words we fling;
So little do we live, so much we miss
So much of love and life and bitter sting.
These lovers, fighters, drinkers, workers, sages . . .
Lovers of life, of hate, of joy and worth.

Here is a dreamer and he sits and dreams
Though no one hears nor lends an ear to hear
He sings of soil and seasons of the year
He looks beyond to see a future time.

I cannot write tonight for the moon is full
And large as a wagon wheel above the timber
I must go out for the world is beautiful
Remember hills stay young, their beauty keeps
Eternally as seasons come and pass.

The Only Place
We Live

Robert E. Gard

**The time is 2:00 a.m. There are lights over at the old Franklin farmhouse. Something is happening. The Franklins are an old, old family around here. Four generations. Dora and Will are the only ones left. They're up late. It isn't like them.**

It was about nine o'clock when Henry came by. I had finished up at the barn, and Dora and me were in the kitchen having a little something before we went to bed. We live in the old Franklin farmhouse; been in our family for more than a hundred years. Guess it was 1948 when the state of Wisconsin gave us a certificate saying that we were a centennial farm. I have been proud of that because my great grandad jerked the stumps out of our fields; made a good farm, good growing land, and deep, deep soil. Rough work, and he near killed Great Grandma Franklin; of course she worked in the fields right alongside of him. Minded the house too; such as they had in those days; and bore the young ones—twelve before she was through. But she outlived him. They are both in the cemetery over on the hill. Same as Dora and me will be someday.

The Franklin Cemetery is kind of a lonesome place, maybe, if you want to look at it that way. But the stars out there are near and easy, and the morning sun strikes the hill earlier than most places. The whole Franklin family lies up there.

Well, about nine o'clock this evening Henry came by, as I said, I heard his old truck rattling into the lane, and went out onto the side porch. Henry drives an old Ford pickup with a closed-in back. His dog, Buster, rides in that. Minute I saw it was Henry I knew what I was in for: a night of following his hound through the timber. Henry has hunting in his blood like most of the Jacksons, crazy for dogs and woods and hunting.

Dora calls from the kitchen, "Who is it, Will?"

And I says, "Oh, it's just Henry Jackson."

And she says, "Oh, dear, then you'll be chasin' in the woods till dawn?"

And I says, "Well, he's hard to say no to."

"I wish Henry'd just not go night runnin' with that hound," Dora says. "And you shouldn't be out all night, you know that."

But when Henry presently came into the kitchen Dora was real nice to him. She made him set down at the table and got some coffee going. Henry has always been our neighbor. He and I grew up together, went to school down at the crossroads together when it was just one room and one teacher. Never forget Henry if you once saw him. Small face, uncommon small, pinched in, scrubbed with short, white hair, and two dog-tails growing out of his nose. Keeps his old bill-cap on all the time; never takes off his cap except for bed. But Dora says she bets he even sleeps with his flaps down. And tonight he has his wind-breaker jacket on, collar stood up, and buttoned around his neck; but you never really notice those things because Henry isn't hardly ever not talk-ing, except when we're alone out in the woods, he don't talk so much. He don't have many teeth, especially in front. He talks loud and smacks his lips, and since he's got no teeth in front, the smacks have a funny hollow sound. Well, Henry is talking and he jollies Dora about being up so late, and she gives it right back to him about lazing in bed all day long and hunting all night.

"Ain't no man of mine going to do that," Dora says, and Henry says, "Well, might make you a better husband if he did; man can learn lots from the night-woods; more'n in the daytime.

"But I got somethin' to tell you, and then Will can decide whether he wants to come out with me tonight. If Dora'll let you that is."

Henry stops to make Dora more curious, which she was, and finally she says, "So you got somethin' to tell?"

"Yes, ma'am, I have."

"You ain't going to tell me and Will that you got a girl friend?"

"What I am going to tell you about I ain't sure I can ever get."

"And what is that?"

"I ain't just sure what it is," Henry answers, "but yestereve I am out in the south field and I hear this thing from over somewheres near the bluff along the river, you know, where 'tis said that gal jumped over, fleeing from the Indians in the early days. Grandpa Jackson told me about that. Bessie's Bluff."

"What'd you hear?" asks Dora.

"I hear an awful shriek and scream; somethin' like a wild woman up there ashriekin', and somethin' like a stuck tomcat; it came acrost the bluffs and the meadows, cuttin' like a knife through the early night, and up yonder on the bluff 'twas day

still, but the stars was comin' out. I never heared a sound like it, just a loud, long screech and then nothin'.

"I knowed there wasn't no woman up there. Why would there be, 'less it was a ghost of that Bessie gal. I don't hold with ghosts myself. But it was somethin', I was sure of that, so the next mornin' I walk over there and climb up part way and come to that ledge, you know, that runs back there about a hundred feet above the river, where the cave is, and the bluff above slanting back a little. Well, up there I seen . . . ."

It was always like that with Henry Jackson. Always it had to be something mysterious or strange out in the woods. Away back, twenty, twenty-five years ago, old Max Carpenter who lived alone those days in a shack up in the bluffs said there was a big animal prowlin' the woods . . . something like a bobcat but away bigger. Nobody but Henry believed Max. Henry believed it then and never forgot, and through the years, Henry made that mysterious beast into a whole lot of sizes and shapes. He was always seeing unusual tracks or marks in the woods, and hearing queer sounds. Henry said quite often that his hound sometimes trailed strange scents in the woods, and Henry could always tell when he did because old Buster bawled in a real different way.

Henry set there at the table drinking coffee and smacking his lips, and Dora set there too, each one waiting out the other.

"All right now," she says. "All right now, Henry Jackson, are you goin' to set there drinkin' my

coffee and smackin' your lips? What in the world did you see up in them hills?''

"Well, I seen a track. Don't be askin' me what the critter was. Just a huge critter, I reckon. A long mark it was in the soft dirt, half humanlike, half animal critter, with long claws. Left the claw marks deep in the dirt. I called old Buster to come and smell of it, and he went near crazy, leapin' and hollerin' like he was scared, but wantin' to tree the critter, too. We never found nothin'. There was only one mark on the ground.''

"There ain't any critter," Dora says. "You told us you seen strange things before, and there ain't never been a critter. There ain't one, that's the reason.''

"No there ain't a critter," I says, but then I felt something in me, too; maybe because I'd heard Henry tell so often about a critter, I kind of half believed him; or maybe it was because I wanted something strange to really exist. Anyway I says to Henry, "That critter is just a dream, Henry.''

"Nope, it ain't. The critter ain't no dream." Henry wiped off his mouth with his jacket sleeve. "Nope, the critter is out there in the dark, amongst trees, and the moon is shinin', and tonight I want to see the wild geese fly acrost the slender moon, which sight I have never seen. And I also want to go night huntin' for the critter.''

"Ain't likely the geese will fly at night," Dora says. "Wild geese rest at night. Fly in the day.''

"But they will fly at night," says Henry. "I've awakened and have heard the wild geese cryin' in the fall and spring. Seein' them up against the moon will be a sight to remember, long as I live.''

Henry has a kind of war on with wild things, though, but like wanting to see wild geese acrost the moon, he has a streak of hope to see something beautiful, too. But he is first of all a hunter and trapper; and only some lately, has he ever talked about preserving and helping wild animals and birds . . . like this mysterious critter, or whatever he thinks is out there; he would catch and kill the critter with pleasure, and would never feel loss that it was gone. To me now, the fanciful existence of a critter is enough. I wouldn't want to kill it or see it killed. Once Henry caught an otter in a trap. The trap wasn't set to catch otter, but for mink; but the otter was taken. Henry didn't think how beautiful the otter swam and played. He saw the otter in the trap and it was his.

I thought about things like that as I put on my boots and jacket. I guess I was glad that Henry had come by because I loved the woods at night, the flicker of a lantern, the voice of the old hound as he ran, and me and Henry walking or running when need be, running through brush and trees. Dora don't see why. And with this dream thing of Henry's, like the flicker of a big shadow seen far away against moonlight, well I am raring to go, that's all, and I say goodnight to Dora and she says, "Will, you get back here by milkin' time. And you be careful! You ain't in no shape for hills at night!''

Well, me and Henry went out into the yard, and Dora shut the door, and we stood there in the yard a little while listening, not speaking a word and the dog in the truck snuffed and let out a couple of bellers, and I looked off acrost the unplowed field over towards the bluff and the woods.

There was a little ravine running down to the foot of the bluffs, and some dark and straight trees along it, and back further a few evergreens up higher; but it's mostly hardwood on the flat around here.

Well, there was a moon hanging there in the east, just a slice of moon, slim, and there wasn't a wind. A perfect sight when something strange surely could happen; and the wild sight of the night set off an urgent feeling in me and I says, "Come on, Henry, let's go."

**Will was shot up during the war. Right after Pearl Harbor he went in. Wasn't married then, and his dad was still alive to run the farm. Will was wounded at Guadalcanal. Took him awhile to get back to farming.**

We get into Henry's truck and head off acrost the field where we will leave the truck and go afoot into the woods. I never tell Henry what it is I love best about nights in the woods. I guess my feeling for going out really is the chance it gives me to remember: things and stories come back in the night-woods. I feel, see, touch the faces of people long gone, my mother, how she nursed me when I was sick, setting there beside the bed in the low chair, singing something old and the night coming up around the Franklin house. All of the past things do come back in the night-woods.

But maybe Henry don't feel things as deep as me.

It's a funny thing: when I am out in the woods at night with a good friend and neighbor like Henry Jackson, it is as if the whole world is mine. I can believe anything I want to, be anyplace, or remember just about anything that happened. And I love to do this. I'm not a great one for daydreaming or dallying during the day, but if there is a small moon over the woods at night, and night sounds all around, something inside of me takes over. I'm me but I'm not me, I am like everybody I ever knew and they are right there beside me. People are mortal, but still, they're not in a way, or not in the way they think they are mortal. When I die I would like to recall all the beautiful things I have seen all my life. That's some kind of immortality; that's the way I figure that folks are in their imaginations. That's why people are immortal, to be able to see and feel all in one moment everything they are, or what the land is, or has been.

We live in a land of small sloughs and marshes in the flatlands back away from the rivers; places of small water, and mud banks and reeds. There are large frogs that rest in against the banks.

Henry and I follow the river's edge to the place where the limestone bluff rises. There is a trail we know well. The trail follows the bluff, then rises, through a crevice, and follows the shoulder up higher and higher, until at the top the trail emerges high above the valley. It's from up here that we can see the far, far shape of the hills and the moon rising. If it were day we could see the bridge across the river.

I have been up here sometimes about dawn, and then, in summer, the bird songs seem to reach out acrost the whole valley. I find it easy to remember bird songs in the early morning. Sometimes I lie in bed beside Dora, thinking of the beautiful sounds I've heard and the sights I've seen. If I should die tomorrow, I couldn't be sorry. I've lived enough for ten people; and I've seen enough of the beautiful things to make me know that the world has all the beauty that a person can stand.

Upriver from our place is a swale, where the river widens out some, and gets very shallow. I guess the glaciers scooped out a kind of shallow hole in there where the river spreads out. There are bog islands and lots of channels in among them. In the early morning I have paddled through the channels in my canoe, listening and watching. I have heard ducks and coots in the tall cattails, and a faraway loon. I have seen kingfishers splash down, and up away ahead, a tall blue heron. I have seen sandhill cranes in there, too, lots of times, and Dad says he saw whooping cranes, white with black wing-tip feathers, standing in there. But I never saw a whooper. They was mostly gone long ago. I have seen the heron rise, then another I hadn't seen. Then another. Three coming over me, and from down below they look immense.

In springtime the whistling swans come to the swale. I one time saw three or four hundred in there, on the wide place just before the river narrows down and flows swifter to the old mill site.

Well, me and Henry are standing up above the valley, and the dog is somewhere on the ridge, we don't know where. And Henry sets down the lantern, and we just hunker down and wait for the dog to call. Henry asks me if I recall the little hollow beside the small bridge. It was a kind of place hid in against the embankment under the Northwestern railroad that runs through there. It was where hobos and tramps drifted off the freights sometimes in the old days to eat and talk. And they had a campfire in there sometimes, and we saw the light of it from our barn while we were doing the milkin'.

**Everybody thought that Will might someday marry Clara Johnson. They were high school sweethearts, but Clara was murdered by those tramps, I guess. That's what they always thought. Will took that mighty hard. With time he married Dora O'Neil.**

Sure is pleasant to lay on a bank above the river on a quiet July afternoon, trying to see the water through the wings of a dragonfly. That will make you cease to remember terrible events.

At the angle of the old fence, in there, in the grass woven together under the rotted boards; down at the sweep of the meadow beyond, down the interlaced roots of the grasses and the ferns; in the whole quiet of the evening there is no movement amongst the grass. But you know that underneath are the field mice; and we walk over their houses, and we can't hear them. The old fox, he hears, though, and pounces quick. But to me the night is not disturbed.

I am thinking of two great horses hitched to the walking plow: the sod-breaker. When I was a boy my dad laid the plow to the stubborn sod in a field that had never before been broke. The settlers came to our parts from New York State, and laid open the earth; but the east meadow they did not break and saved that for a prairie pasture. And when my father hitched up that morning to go to the field, the blacks, the Percherons, the harness studded with brass, the thick black tugs, well oiled, and clinking chains fast to the doubletrees and clevis . . . the horses dragged the heavy plow side down, around the pasture track. Straightened at the sod's edge, pulled back and the handles firm into my father's hands, he spoke to them:

"Now my friends, we will do it as they did when they came here in 1848. Now we will hear and see and feel what it was like to turn the first sod."

They were like steeds of the old gods, I guess, and the plow cut down into the sod, and the strip ribboned out flat behind. My father walked in the clean furrow.

Now, on the bluff's edge I see and feel the way the plow went; the pull and tear of it, and the heartbreaking severing sound of the roots: smell the earth not turned for a thousand years, or never. The smell is mouldy, clean, severed, faintly pungent, amoniac, small gasses released, the smell of root juice. The sound: grunt of the black horses, the low voice of my father guiding, urging, impelling, restraining. The flick of tail hair, the light brush of the wind, the birds crowding in the furrow behind. Yes, there were blackbirds, star-

lings, crows, sparrows, feeding on what had been opened up to the sky. Upon me was the heat of the morning sun, the filter of the seasons, and my mother's voice from the field edge later; she was there with a lunch for us. I, too small to labor, but not too little to follow the furrow and remember.

**Everybody likes Will Franklin. He would just do anything for you. Some neighbors are that way. They seem to know when you need a friend to help. Will is about the best-liked farmer in the whole valley even if he isn't the best farmer. Folks look up to him and Dora, they're kind of in on everything. Will and Dora didn't get married till Will came home from the war. She got him on his feet, but Will hasn't ever been real strong.**

Some folks around here have lots of pictures and pretty wallpaper on their living room and bedroom walls. But some farmers still have nothing to make the room look more like home. It used to be more that way, there was hardly a picture anywhere; a few farmhouses had a picture of the horse fair; or maybe a colored picture of Jesus. And there were usually calendars stuck up in the kitchen with maybe a snowy scene like a farmer coming home and his house lit up, warm and homey, and the sun just sinking down. That was a favorite, same as animal pictures; Stag at Bay was a good one.

Nowadays, though, there are really nice pictures in most houses, and quite a few have ones painted by folks right around home. I like those 'specially well, because they are about scenes we all know: cows, farmhouses, old wells and windmills, or an old blacksmith shop, maybe. Things like that.

But about the only decoration in Henry's house is the round oak stove. I tell you it is hard to find an object more friendly than an old stove that's been burned for fifty winters or more, to heat up a farmhouse living room. And the way they were decorated: filigree work at the top, all in nickel, with a bell up high against the stovepipe, and scrollwork lower down sweeping up to a whole nickel foot-ring that went clean around the stove. Filigree work on the front stove door, too, and a nickel-plated handle, and best of all that wide rim around the bottom where a man could warm his frosted feet after coming in from the barn on a January day. A man could put his booted feet on the rim, and then the manure would begin to get hot, and the smell of barn would waft around in the house. But nobody minded, I suppose, because comfort came from the stove and belonged to everybody.

On the lip of the bluff we could see down, down, down and acrost in the faint moonlight. Above us there were rustles of a few leaves still left on the oaks, and far acrost the valley the ghost-white of the wall of rock rose high and became fainter as the white moon began to slip away. Away off to the left of us old Buster gave tongue once, and was still.

We sat on the earth; I backed against the oak, and Henry hunkered down on the flat rock, slippery down to the edge of the void. I raised up our electric lantern a little, and shone it over acrost the valley. The faint gleam of the light never reached the far rocks. It flickered and was lost.

"Buster hasn't found the critter yet," says Henry. "If Buster had found trace of the critter he'd be bellerin' and mouthin'. Could hear him ten mile. Buster hasn't found nothin' yet."

"There ain't a critter but in a dream," I says.

"There is a critter, and we'll see it tonight," Henry says positive.

But I am not thinking about the critter. I am thinking about how the dim-lighted swatches of the bare earth acrost the valley look like patches of snow . . . faint I imagine with no mantrack on it No men here at all. Nothing about men. Just as it was in the beginning, when earth and rock and snow was all there was.

The old hound bays again, closer, it seems to me, and Henry puts up his hand to his ear.

"I believe Buster is runnin' something. And the way he is tonguin', it ain't no coon."

The voice of the hound was certainly different, sharper, almost fearful. But I wasn't solely listening to the dog. I suppose I have heard all sorts of sounds at night. I dwell and revel in sounds and in the fruit of all the senses. Every countryman does. He is tuned to hear, to sense, and his nostrils and ears try out the sounds and smells of the night always; not consciously, but the scent, the sound of cattle, the night-rising mists from earth, the sounds from trees, of wind, of water, the scurry of small animals, of more odorous skunks, of fern, of wild apples, the far sounds made by men and machines, knowledge of the sounds within hollows of rock, a calling woman far away, a man's muted voice in answer, the soft low of a milk cow, sound of wings, small and large, sound of the wild geese calling from the marsh, an owl in the dark, the cry of a small thing suddenly seized, a flicker of bats, the nighthawk boom, the train rumble on the trestle over the marsh: yes, all of this, all, all and more.

The marsh lies below the Franklin farm, running on south, bottomless, so the engineers once said when they strove to put a roadbed through it. But the rails ran on a trestle. They drove the piles down and down and the track was finally spanned on the oaken bridge. The train, in the old days, went slow across the trestle; the trembling of earth, muted by the soft muck of the marsh, we felt in the barnyard. And then the whistle of the steam locomotive, first faint, from the crossing five miles east, then closer and closer, then loud as it came onto the trestle, then the sound of going, going, and so lost, lost in the reaches of the dark beyond the marsh.

First, when the fall was in, and the wild geese were resting upon the marsh, roosting in the night upon the marsh waters, floating, with the low sounds now and again, the source of the sounds unseen, and then far away, the train and in memory the sight of the ghost-birds floating away. There was a dead tree near the beginning of the marsh trestle, and back in and among the marsh waters the islands of peat, and the cattails with dry thrust and rustle, their heads brown above the marsh.

Along in spring the pussy willows bud branches in the swale below the old Ferris barn. Dora waits for that day all the winter, and the time that the white trilliums open out in the woods.

But me, I love the winter, too, and the way the old fences struggle downhill, and mark the efforts of them who laid out this country.

**Will and Henry Jackson have always been good friends. Henry is more easygoing than Will, of course, and Henry's place is kind of a dump-heap. Henry has always been more interested in hunting and fishing than farming. Will used to go over to help with the harvest, but Henry doesn't bother putting in crops anymore. He's got a few cows, and raises a little hay. But he spends most of his time out in the woods.**

There isn't any end to memories and thoughts in the night-woods; they come and slip and linger on and are lost. I have wandered through these woods in sunlight and in dark; I, the hunter, gun under arm, down the hillsides terraced, natural, not man-made, but there are circles of the grass terraces running on downhill, and I stepping carefully down, aiming towards the large birch. I saw the big buck near that tree one autumn morning, motionless with head high, looking out towards me; in the dawn so much larger than life. I stood and waited for him to vanish, the ghost deer, but he would not. I couldn't even lift the gun. There was a mysterious power came flowing from him that prevented me. Another time I would have shot him, and buried my hands and arms in his blood and entrails but not now. I lifted my arm, and he wheeled, tail flashed, he disappeared. I never pass that way without remembering the mighty buck. I fear that he was shot that Thanksgiving time, the kill was heavy, but you cannot recognize your friend the spirit buck, when he lies dead upon leaves.

Some things I feel strong about. The old folks in our neighborhood. John Morgan was eighty-five last June. Related to Dora on her mother's side. Dora feels she ought to do for John, but he will have no help. Lives alone and cuts his own firewood; pulls it in from the woods on a sled; says no fire will warm his bones but made from woods-cut oak. John's brother, Max, lived with him till he died. Both was doughboys in World War I. Max was younger; not sturdy as John. Max got hung up in a barbed-wire fence when he was going on seventy. Was trying to crawl through between the wires. Hung there in twenty below cold and froze to death. Tragedies of the country and tragedies of getting old I suppose. But age don't bother old John at all, seems like.

**Seems like Will just didn't want to do anything for fun of late years except fuss around with wild things. He had a pen of wild geese for awhile, and he kept that swale down on the Franklin Farm like a kind of refuge for wild things. He was thinking all the time.**

Henry and I listen awhile to the sounds of the night. The hound is not baying now. He is out there somewhere, but there is no sound from him. Henry, though, is not one to keep silent long. There is a smacking sound, and I know that he is about to spit out words.

"Now I ain't never seen the critter, but I knowed them as have. I knowed two fishermen was traveling along a timber road, as they said, in the early light; not hurryin' since they knowed well where they was headed. And as they was toolin' a model T Ford around a curve they seen something there in the gray. It was a mighty beast, or somethin' like a beast that leapt out from the roadside, and in the middle of the roadway it stood, looking down the road to where they was acomin'. It was a yellowish thing, they said, big as a lumberwagon, and it lingered there in the road and watched while they stopped the Ford, and they were afeared to get out. But the critter never came for the car, and gave a great leap and bounce and clear away over the roadside brush, like a gray mist of cloud, they said, and off into timber. But they was afeared to go after it, though they had a shotgun in the Ford; but they creeped up there finally to look for spoor and there in the road they seen a huge track, and it was just the same, as they told about it, as the print I seen on the bluffs; the very same. The critter is out there all right, and I mean to catch it.

"Oh, if it was but winter now, and deep snow. The white lace of a mornin' of snow," Henry cries, "and there in the whole white pile of the field there ain't nothing to mess the snow until there comes a hell of a scream, and the critter rises up out of the snowy nothin'. The hounds see it, and they take in after; and at the edge of the field they come upon it, and there is a fling of snow and a squall and a bawl, and there is snow and things flashin' and cryin' and the snow is turnin' to red; and the great critter jumps for the trees, but the mighty black hounds have him, and there under the trees the critter is quiet. The hell hounds have killed it."

"Or the critter has killed the hounds," I say. "Or might if the critter was more'n just a dream."

Down the way the fence posts march, each with a cap of white, and the barn beyond with the spread white roof, and beyond up the slope the junipers planted by the birds struggle to capture the hillside. It is lonely and white, and afar off there is a small darkness where the timbered ridge begins.

It is over here that Pa and I will cut down the great basswood. Away up, above the first spread of limb, there is a hole into the tree. I climbed to it a few times when I was a boy and thrust a stick down hoping to poke an animal within. Now, I know that a coon lives there, and as Pa and I knock about on the trunk, cutting a deep notch so that the tree will fall away from the deep down-slope, I hope that the coon, if he is inside will hear and depart. He does not, and we put the cross-cut to the trunk, Pa and I at the ends, and we saw through the great old trunk until it cracks and sways and Pa yells "Timber!" and we jump away from it. The tree thunders to the earth and I think: he will have a terrible ride; and the hole in the tree lies turned up to the sky. No raccoon's nose emerges and I say, "Well, the coon wasn't at home."

"And just as well," says Pa.

But as we saw the basswood up, in lengths for splitting, we find the coon. He lies inside the trunk and Pa says, "I guess he never wanted to leave home."

Henry said we ought to move, to chase on up the slope, or down, if Buster called from that way. But we do not hurry. These are night excursions to dream and chatter. We both know it, and Henry waits for Buster to bay while I listen for other kinds of sounds.

Sounds, as I said, are long in memory; the voice of the Canada geese as they migrate through above our pasture in November, high against the dark wind and their voices barely heard against the sky. And I have watched the hawks, high, so high, they are nearly lost at the tips of clouds; then down, their dive and rush and swoop, and a wild cry. I have heard no cry more wild than hawks.

There are other screams than just of hawks. Was a Sunday morning, I remember, and I was out in the woods exploring for the first spring flowers. It's a sad memory; like I was all alone with a whisper. I was in the woods, walking pretty quiet, because all the woods was so quiet; and of a sudden I heard this scream, loud and terrible. I stopped and looked, awful scared, because Pa had told me in those childhood days, that there might be fearsome things in the deep woods . . . to keep me from running away and getting lost, I guess. But then the scream came again, and again and again. I thought it came from behind a rotting log. I saw something move at the end of the log, black and low in the old leaves. Then the scream again. I saw a big black snake had a young rabbit, wasn't hardly more'n a baby, and it was the rabbit makin' the screams. I wouldn't have ever guessed that a small rabbit could scream so loud. The snake had the rabbit in its mouth. I picked up a stick, but I was trembling so's I could hardly stand; it was all a shock to me, for I knew that snakes ate rabbits, but I never heard the screams before. I guess I was going to try to kill the snake, but sudden the

snake was gone, and the rabbit was gone. I ran home feeling sick. Ma said it was the way things were, when I told her, but that didn't make me feel any better. I never do see a black snake today without thinking of that.

Some said Will never really was the same after the war. Was more lonely and harder to talk with. He was the one who fought so hard against the engineers when they wanted to build the dam up the river. Will lost the fight. Folks around here couldn't see but that the dam would make things better, stop the floods and all; but maybe Will was right in some ways. Will lost a few friends in that battle.

I'm not a real fancier of snakes, but still, I have learned to like them some. They are kind of beautiful, and they fit in with the rocks and the woods and the grass. I don't hold with killing snakes just because they are snakes. The hills are full of rattlers. I've seen them many a time up in the high rocks, laying out, liking the sun.

Besides deer, there aren't any large wild animals in our parts now, except them that are dreamed about by Henry. There isn't any strange critter loose in these woods. Henry dreams of unusual things to make his own life more interesting. But there are plenty of coons. And we have some beaver along the river. Never used to be any, and possums and skunks more'n ever. And the rabbits go up and down; but there was a large crop of rabbits last year. They add something beautiful. Ever see a pretty cottontail bust up out of a snowbank where the snow has covered the weeds and tall grass, and has sort of bent them down? That's what I mean, a good hiding place, and warm in there. You walk acrost places like that, edge of a marsh, or side of a meadow, near to the fence; or along an old hedgerow. You are not looking to shoot a rabbit necessarily, but you love to see them bust out of the snow. It is a beautiful sight, like a small explosion, and off he goes acrost the slope near the little stream; and the stream isn't frozen yet, though there is snow piled all along the banks, and the dark water. Away off there he goes, leaping, brown against the white, and a hunter would think, I guess, now I could roll him. Just there. But I never like to think that way. I would rather think: Wonderful, beautiful! I hope he runs forever. Well, we had plenty of rabbit stews at the First Baptist Church. Big crowds! Wild rabbits, hunted and killed and hung out to freeze by the side door of the church. Rabbit stew and hot baking-powder biscuits! A fine combination and I could eat some right now, except that I love the wild rabbits unharmed nowadays. It is so beautiful to watch them in winter.

Henry is talking about things he has caught and killed. "I hunted bobcats and lynxes and I hunted me a wolverine once. Killed a few thousand creatures. And once I chased up mountain cats out West, up in high country. Wanted to get in real close. I seen a big cat but once, that was all. I been afraid once or twice too. And I swear I'd be afraid if we was to come up onto the critter. Killin' him is somethin' I want, but I don't want, too. It's a kind of a holy fear like wanting to go to church but being afraid to.

"Now listen! There goes old Buster. Maybe he has started up the critter. The critter has a strong scent for a trailing hound. Listen to him holler! We better set out to follow. If we come up to the critter and take it, we will have our pictures in the paper. We could be standing there under a tree and the critter strung up by the hind legs, and you and me and Buster looking proud. Can't figure out where a critter would hide. Where would a big beast live? In a cave? Under a big rock? Where? And what is a critter eating? Deer? Well, there are plenty of deer around in the hills this year. Seen a whole herd come out just yesterday at the edge of the forty. Twenty, maybe. They weren't scared a bit. Wasn't as if there was a critter trailing them. They would know about a critter all right. You ain't really believin' in the critter are you?"

"I believe in no critter."

Great grandpa was a York Stater. He came from that hill country in western York State, somewhere around a place called Fredonia, and he walked out to the new state carrying all he had on his back. Great grandpa said that his friend and neighbor, who came out with him, was a prophet of strange things to come. He was foretelling the end of the world near every mile, great grandpa said, and carried a long staff of locust wood. He told how in 1843 he held with the Millerites, and how they knew what day the world would come to its end in a thundering burst of flame and smoke. Come the day, he said, the Millerites climbed to hilltops or up into trees, and waited for the angels to fly in and bear them off to heaven. That time the angels didn't come, but great grandpa's neighbor said the day would arrive, he hadn't given up on it, when terrible fire would consume all but the faithful—them that were ready and waiting on the high places. When these two York Staters came into the new homeland great grandpa took up his homestead on the prairie, out amongst the oak openings, where the breaking of new land was easier. But his neighbor went direct to a hilltop and there he took out the land for his home. And there where he had cleared a little spot, great grandpa said, the Millerite man jammed his tall staff of locust wood into the earth to remind him that he was humble and had no wagon to ride in. Great grandpa said it was true that his neighbor's staff took root and grew to a great locust tree; and that under it he sat on many Sunday afternoons

when he was an old man, and told about the coming end of the world in fire and smoke.

This neighbor, this prophet of olden times, who saw the world ending when the sun got too hot to bear, would have no horse-drawn implements to cut the grain. This he did himself with scythe and cradle until he was old, and at evening his old wife brought bread to the field, and in the setting sun they would stand together bowed in prayer. Great grandpa said he saw them that way many a time. Was a picture hung in our country school: two old people with heads bared to the setting sun, praying together. And, great grandpa said, it was a surely calm and beautiful sight those two old neighbors, with piles of yellow hand-cut grain, and the hills risin' up around the field.

**Will always was a homebody. He never was happy anywhere else, but around here. As I said, Will was shot up pretty bad in World War II, but you never hear him talk about that. He always likes to wander around alone in the fields and woods. I guess he isn't really much of a farmer, not lazy, but interested in too many things, I guess.**

Great grandpa was an old, old man when I sat beside of him in the yard to hear him spin stories about his life. He rocked and spit from an old Boston rocker that his wife had brought to their home when they were married. He said he never sat in any other chair if he could avoid it. Sat there and rocked and talked. Kept an old cane always in his right hand and jammed it at the floor when he was making a strong argument. He said America was strong because the pioneers were strong, and filling up the country with strength and energy. In his late nineties he lived just to talk and dream. He said that when his own boy, my grandpa, was sixteen, he sent him out to the West to see and feel what the new country was like. Great grandpa thought the whole part of the West was covered with tall prairie grass, but the boy came back and told how lots of the prairie was already gone and plows breaking it up everyplace. The old man said he knew then that was a bad thing, and that the whole fertile land would sometime drift away on the winds.

Day after day great grandpa sat there and rocked; and his mind would begin to recall things, and I was glad to sit on the stoop and listen. He was a wonderful old man, very tall and straight. He would recall how it was when he came home from the Civil War. Great grandpa had been to war four years; great grandma had some help from the neighbors, and worked the home land as well as she could, but she couldn't hardly swing the heavy grain cradle and great grandpa told how she must have suffered out in the fields, no man to help her and only one horse. They raised wheat those early years, because it was the big cash crop and needed in the war. But then one day, late afternoon, grandpa and his ma were out in the yard at the side of the little white house, and they saw, away down the road, somebody coming. They stood there watching, and sudden his ma shoved the damp hair away from her eyes and cried out, "It's him! It's Tom!" and they began to run down the dirt road and the faraway figure began to run up towards them, and grandpa said he would never forget how his pa looked as he climbed the hill, tall and thin, with the blue uniform looking too big for him. His pa's hair was long and hung to his shoulders and he was wearing a soldier's cap that was too little for him. And then grandpa said his pa grabbed up his wife and son all in one hug and they set there in the road a long, long while, all of them holding onto each other and crying for happiness and joy.

You probably know how it is: the pictures that will come into a person's mind, as if a whole life is drifting past, just a person's memory flowing backwards like a great stream that runs and runs and never stops. That's the way it is with me; most anything will come crowding acrost my mind, especially when it's nighttime and quiet, like now, and when Henry and me are listening for the baying of a hound. That is the time for memories to come pushing around in my head. And when I am thinking about how great grandpa came home from the Civil War, I get to remembering what they said about Dick Walters coming home from World War I. That was a terrible war, worse than most folks think about now, I guess. They have forgotten what remarkable changes were forced on us after that war that changed our lives. But there are old fellows around still who remember plenty how it was. It is when these old World War I veterans get together that they begin to tell about how patriotic everybody was in 1917, and how they got to supposing that any neighbor with a German name was a spy. Most of the young men around here went off to the war; and some came drifting back after it was over. A few of them were in terrible shape, too. Like Dick.

Dick lived then and still does, a mile west of us Franklins. He was just a doughboy in the war, was real bad shell-shocked, and came home a wreck; wouldn't talk to anybody, wouldn't laugh or smile, just set in a chair in the yard, or rocked in the old rocking chair on the porch, gazing out acrost the land, not really seeing anything at all, much as

anybody could tell. I never knew much about what happened, because I was younger then, of course, younger than Dick, I mean, and I wasn't overmuch interested in Dick or his troubles. But later on when the story got going around, and when the old-timers would get together in the thirties or the forties when World War II was roaring, they would tell it, and I was interested then, all right.

Lantern light in the barn, or on a summer's night out under the trees after a long day in the hayfield they would sometimes tell about Dick; and if Dick was there he'd maybe add a few remarks about himself. He wasn't self-conscious or anything. Dick knew what he went through and was proud of it; but old Syl McDonald would usually begin by telling how the Armistice was declared while he was drunk, and when he got back to the lines his outfit had been moved. He told a long story with a lot of variations.

And Syl would maybe relate how he got back home before Dick Walters, back to this home country, and he said he saw Dick walking up the hill to the Walters farmhouse one rainy day in April 1919. Dick was in his uniform, with his head down, slogging along in the wet and mud, almost as if he was still a doughboy over in France.

"Hadn't of been for Grandma Walters," Syl would say, "I guess Dick wouldn't of ever pulled out of it."

And if Dick was there he'd always holler, "No I wouldn't of."

"You talk about them modern psychologists," Syl would say, "Well, Grandma had 'em all beat. She seen right away that Dick was still living over all those awful days of battle, and she recalled that her husband, old Sam Walters, was just the same when he come home from the Civil War, and set still out in the yard or wandered around the barn and fields without sayin' a word. Grandma said she pulled Sam out of that by getting him to go with her down by the crick, and walk through every step of the Battle of Shiloh step-by-step, same as she heard it told about from other Union veterans. Made old Sam walk through that battle with her, and when the make-believe battle was over he got to telling about his part in it, just what he had done and all, and he talked most of a whole day, and by gosh that evening Sam come up to the barn and got a milkin' stool and pailed six cows, and forked down the hay and was cured, I guess. And then Grandma done the same for Dick, her grandson, when he come home from Europe."

Dick would holler, "Yes she did!"

"Well one day about in August 1919, Grandma got old Dick to take a walk with her, down by the crick, same as she done with Sam, and she got Dick to a place where she could get him kind of interested in the stories she had to tell about the Battle of Shiloh. And by gosh, she got Dick to fight out the Battle of Shiloh for her, just like she did with Sam, and after they had finished the Battle of Shiloh, and Grandma had told Dick she could hear the wagons rumbling away, and the pitiful cries of those wounded, and the way night was coming down on the Shiloh battlefield . . ."

"And the way Grandpa was feeling then," says Dick, "all empty and shot out, and not caring about a thing."

"And by gosh," says Syl, "old Dick begins to talk about the Battle of the Argonne Forest, where he had such a terrible time, and was left on the field for dead . . . just laid there shocked senseless. Dick just talked and talked. It just come apourin' out, all of it, all about the hellish noise, the terrible smoke, the way the trees was all shot to pieces, the dark clouds . . . . Seemed like, when he was telling it to Grandma, he could recall it all. And right there he got over his trouble, whatever it was, and he never felt real poorly again.

"I never did!" yells Dick.

"Dick walked home from the crick and the two battles that afternoon with Grandma and they got the milk cows into the barn, just the two of them, the old lady and the doughboy, and Dick gets a pail and a three-legged milkin' stool and does the milkin', and they had a big dinner and a kind of party that night. Dick was made whole by Grandma Walters."

"Ain't many now like old Grandma Walters," says Henry. Because I had been telling the story out loud, I never even knew I was talking, or that Henry was listening.

**If Will's pa hadn't left some money I don't rightly know how well Will would of got along. I guess Will is more of a poet. He writes verses folks say. I never read any of them. He is a funny kind of fellow, and I guess Dora is the real strength in that house; but everybody likes both of them.**

This land of ours is peaceful; sometimes my soul seems to float on the river. When I walk along our road in the morning in winter, just when the sun is coming up, the trees look so black against the morning sky. I always wished I could tell how deep that makes me feel.

When the settlers came to these parts there were lots of great oaks; all around and amongst them were the openings in the prairie. It was here that my York State folks broke new ground and made a home; on the prairie among the oak openings. I wish I could have seen the prairie grass then, and the plants and flowers that have all disappeared now; well, there is one little piece of original prairie left, over beside the railroad. Some flowers are growing there that are no place else.

But in the woods in spring the blossoms stare out everyplace. I go out in the woods in spring and stand and watch and listen. I soak it all in. Dora likes her potted plants and flowers. There is something about a potted flowering plant that is beautiful too, also something of death and rarity, all of those things, Dora says.

You've seen the dark patterns of tree shadows on a bright day in July? They lie clean acrost the pasture as evening comes on.

Once in a long while we still see an eagle around here in the deep, deep July sky. Nested down along the river. Bald eagles; and even now, sometimes in the spring, when the geese are migrating north, we will see a golden eagle. They say a golden will take a goose in flight. I've never seen it.

I expect that the way I feel has a lot to do with the way we worked when I was a kid. The feel of summer, August, when the whole country is sort of hazy, sun-filled but hazy and still. Wasn't for the traffic you can hear faint, over on the highway, you wouldn't notice much but the natural sounds on an August afternoon. Then even the buzz of a fly sounds awful loud. And recalling the way we loaded hay on the haywagon, two of us pitching it up and one loading on the wagon; both of us hay pitchers, my brother and me; strong country boys, we would get our pitchforks into the hay bunched up by the raker, and together we'd lift and swing the whole bunch onto the wagon. No matter how high the load we'd heave it up. And when the load got top-heavy, somehow we'd climb up on it from the rack at the rear, and ride to the stack or the barn. The load seemed likely to scrape the sky; at least it was that way laying on your back staring up as the wagon jolted along over the rough road. Sky, clouds and the round hills, south end of the valley. It was all hay smell and movement, sky, clouds, heat too, and peace like I have never since known. Now, of course, everything is all different. They bale and roll the hay and let it lay in the field, and one man can about accomplish it. But with horses and a haywagon and three or four husky young fellows, joyful, strong, and the juice of life flowing deep inside, and heavy work in the sun, these things I have never forgot.

You ever see the full moon rise over a far-off hill, and you are standing over acrost, on the other side of the valley? Well, there is a river down below the hill, and you can see the river like a little white thread off there, and this side of the river are the pines and cedars. There are a lot of cedars on the hillside and they look real tall against the moon. Only the last thirty years the cedars have come. Down this side of the river is the marsh; not much good for farming. Used to be a gang of horse thieves in there in the olden days. Had them a shack and kept stolen horses, painted the faces of the blaze-faced ones; owner hardly ever recognized his own. But that was a long, long time ago. The marsh will never be the same. They built the dam away up the river, and there is hardly ever any floodtime now. Water levels have all been changed. But the moon coming up over the hill, that's the same as it was when I was a boy. Kind of wish it could always be night so I could remember better how things were. The changes that have hurt the land have hurt me too.

These midland rivers are not as peaceful as they seem. In the old floodtimes they spread out acrost the whole valley. The rivers are very old and the banks are low, the bottoms are mud, the fish —catfish or carp, suckers, sunfish and bluegills, bullheads and buffalo. A few bass, once in a while a northern pike. Once there was sturgeon here. No longer. Mink travel along the water to hunt, and the coon tracks are everywhere etched in the mud. But these low-bank rivers were dangerous when they swelled. Farmers had to watch their cattle. When the flood water receded the grasses lay thick encrusted with the river mud.

Will and Dora don't have any kids. Guess they couldn't. Been a Franklin living on that farm since 1848. While back, Will got real interested in the Franklin family and went to the big library at Madison and got some help finding out about them. Found out how they came from Pennsylvania to New York State after the Revolution and on out here. Will was sure fond of telling about his grandpa and great grandpa. He had his roots deep in this land, and always wanted a kid to leave the farm to. Well, Dora has some relatives. Farm'll go to them I suppose. But the place will always be the old Franklin farm to us folks around here.

"Listen, listen," Henry cries, and I thought he was hearing the hound, but it was another sound in the luminous sky. It came from the north and east; it was a low sound with a common, rolling, and fluctuant note. The sound was of a quality both high and low, and as the sound neared it became one voice and many, faintly and louder and swelling and fading. It was the call of wild geese in the night sky; and behind them the moon glimmered on their wingtips. We saw both their reality and shadow. We saw the volume of their flight, and the mystery of their calling filled the entire valley. We saw dimly and imagined their shapes. I uttered no sound. I was engulfed in a sky filled with the wild beauty of night-migrating birds. I heard Henry say, "I'd like to be among 'em." But with Henry you don't know exactly what he means.

We watched as the V flights crossed the moon. I could feel my spirit dividing to join the geese, to be borne with them through the cold air. I was purified by sound and night.

Henry said we ought to move, that the dog would give tongue soon again; and presently Buster's howl flowed from somewhere, we thought below us, then again it sounded and it was from above. We waited and its sound was upslope we were sure. "He's heading for the bluff," Henry cried; and we pushed away at the brush and hurried upward, Henry first, and I soon after him, the light wavered among the trunks. I could not keep up with Henry. It was always the same when we went out at night; Henry is first, for he is anxious to catch up to the dog and the quarry.

"Faster," cries Henry. "Come faster! I believe Buster has treed the critter!"

We climb upward, then the dog calls from below us and we drop down and down to the valley. We strike the valley bottom, and the small, cold stream; it flows from a spring and in April, watercress is here, crisp for gathering. The stream is narrow. We cross without caring and the water is above our boots. In the night, dark shapes in flickering light, the trees. In autumn I came here alone many times; once when I had been away for years, the war in the Pacific, and returning saw the twisting trees upon the grassy bank. There was a tint of evening sun, and among the mysterious trees I lived the loneliness of homecoming.

"The critter is treed!" cries Henry, and now from the hill to the west comes Buster's howl, again and again. We leave the stream and hurry up the slope again. My feet are wet.

"The bluff," Henry cries.

The bluff is there. The dog is there, clawing up against the yellow rock, his legs are spread and into the dark above Buster casts wild cries.

"Up there, up there somewhere on the bluff. That's where the critter is. That's where I found the critter's track! The cave up there!"

The cave is high near the top of the bluff. Henry and I puff up along the old trail, following the dog, climbing, clinging to shrubs and brush and trunks of small trees rooted into the rock walls.

"Somethin' up there, certain," mutters Henry. "The critter, I'm thinkin'."

If it is the critter, up above, if he is real, he is still there for there is no other way to get to the cave. He is there, and if he comes down we will all meet, right here on this ledge.

But nothing comes and we keep on climbing. We find the dog and he is unable to scale the final cliff. After helping the dog to scramble in the dark, we are at the top, at the cave mouth. Buster bays, looks into the mouth of the dark and when Henry puts the light on him, Buster hollers louder and circles Henry's legs, comes back to the mouth of the cave, enters, backs out and enters again, his growls are frightened and I realize that there may indeed be something more within the cave than a frightened small animal.

"The kill," Henry says.

"Let it alone, whatever it may be," I say.

"Death," Henry says.

"Let it live."

"Our night hunt always ends when somethin' dies! The critter must be caught and killed."

I love the things that are free and wild. I've hunted deer, but I never liked it very much when they were slaughtered. I love the wild, free creatures, and think of them as hungry and cold and warm and free and fearful and peaceful: about the same as I myself do and feel. If there is a critter, even in Henry's imagination, I do not want it to perish. I want to imagine the strength of the creature, see it splendid and tawny and perfect. I remember a magnificent stallion I once saw when he reared against the sky, and it was as though the whole world was not as big and beautiful and terrible as the great horse. And if there is to be a moment of death, I wish to see it alone. I want to see and to marvel by myself. I do not want Henry to see what I see and so I say to Henry, "I will go alone into the cave and find the critter if he is there."

He doesn't try to stop me at all. He says nothing as I take the light from him, turn the beam of the light into the cave. I do not see anything because the cave has a turning a few feet in from the mouth, but there is a definite and wild odor. Henry is suddenly scrabbling in the earth at the mouth of the cave, crying that the critter will come at me in the dark. I have never before seen Henry afraid.

I call to Henry to hold back the dog, and I enter

deeper into the cave and stooping, turn the corner; for I know that the cave is not deep.

I shine the light. There is nothing at the end of the cave. I stand, listening, awaiting the beautiful thing that I know now is to happen. Yet nothing happens. I wait. I turn and then there is something. It comes at me and overcomes me like the night and the geese acrost the moon. It is the wind on the hillside, and the blooming of the trilliums in the spring woods. It is the beauty and grace of all creatures, and the slow sweep of the river. It is the land and the essence of the toil of pioneers. It is of the goodness and the sweetness of living. Have I encountered the critter? I do not know.

Again I return to the cave's mouth. I shine my light here and there among the rocks. Henry is gone. Buster is gone. I am alone.

I put out the light and listen. I think I hear the sound of geese in the night, very faintly and the sound is gone.

The lights are going out now over at the old Franklin place. Been more'n an hour since I heard the news. Poor Will, going like that up in the bluffs. I guess they had a time getting him down; you would wish he'd been home in bed. Wasn't in any shape to go out in the hills at night with Henry Jackson. Dora would have wanted him at home. But he's gone now. It'll be a lonely time for her without Will. But they'll bring him back to the hill with the other Franklins. There won't be a Franklin on the farm; but that's the way it is with these old families. And now Dora's gone to bed. She's put out the lights.

# COLOPHON

The text of this book is set in 12-point Korinna,
with 2-point leading for the prose sections,
and 4-point leading for the poetry.
The text was composed and printed by
Straus Printing and Publishing, Madison, Wisconsin,
on 80# Mountie Matte.
The endpaper is Multicolor Antique Thistle.
The book was bound at
Worzalla Publishing, Stevens Point, Wisconsin,
in Holliston Buckram, English Finish.